FOUNDATIONS OF THE
PHILOSOPHY OF VALUE

FOUNDATIONS OF THE PHILOSOPHY OF VALUE

AN EXAMINATION OF VALUE AND VALUE THEORIES

BY

H. OSBORNE

CAMBRIDGE

AT THE UNIVERSITY PRESS

1933

CAMBRIDGE
UNIVERSITY PRESS

University Printing House, Cambridge CB2 8BS, United Kingdom

Cambridge University Press is part of the University of Cambridge.

It furthers the University's mission by disseminating knowledge in the pursuit of education, learning and research at the highest international levels of excellence.

www.cambridge.org
Information on this title: www.cambridge.org/9781316626054

© Cambridge University Press 1933

First published 1933
First paperback edition 2016

A catalogue record for this publication is available from the British Library

ISBN 978-1-316-62605-4 Paperback

For
P. I. O.

PREFACE

THIS book has developed from a dissertation written at Cambridge in 1929. Owing to the importunity of external circumstances I have been able to devote myself but rarely and spasmodically to philosophical thought since that time. But my convictions on the Philosophy of Value have matured almost unconsciously to myself during this period, until I felt that the time had come for their formulation, lest ceasing to develop further they should become obscured. I regard the present formulation as a stage for further advance. While I do not regard the opinions expressed in it as final, I do not expect to depart radically from them. The actual writing was compressed into three weeks, the evenings alone of which were available, at a time when access to libraries was barred. I can only apologise to my readers for the deficiencies which of necessity remain in a work produced in these conditions.

My thanks are due to the editors of *Mind* and the *Journal of Philosophy* for permission to reproduce portions of articles from those periodicals.

Finally, I would acknowledge the immeasurable debt I owe to those who guided my studies in philosophy. What little I have achieved I owe entirely to the kind and patient teaching of Dr F. R. Tennant, to the wise and inspiring conversation of Dr Oman, and to the lectures of Dr Broad.

H. OSBORNE

CAMBRIDGE
September 1932

CONTENTS

C H. VON EHRENFELS wrote in the introduction
to his *System der Werttheorie* (1897): "Seit den
griechischen und römischen Ethikern des Alter-
tums hat es wohl keine Zeit gegeben, in welcher die
Werttheorie, únd was an Problemen sachlich mit ihr
zusammenhängt, so sehr im Blickfelde der allgemeinen
Aufmerksamkeit gestanden wäre, wie gegenwärtig".
Dr F. C. S. Schiller somewhere remarks that the
emergence and elaboration of Philosophy of Value is
destined to be regarded as the peculiar contribution of
our age to the development of philosophy. Indeed it is
not too much to assert that general metaphysics can no
longer be treated in divorce from considerations of
Value. Theory of Value is now a no less necessary part of
the equipment of every competent philosopher, than is
epistemology.

It is usual to trace back to Kant the emergence of
Value as an independent concept forming the subject-
matter of a special branch of philosophy. In his *Philosophy of Religion* Höffding says: "We are indebted to
Kant's philosophy for the independence of the problem
of value as apart from the problem of knowledge. He
taught us to distinguish between valuation and explanation". Kemp Smith writes in the introduction to his
Commentary on the Critique of Pure Reason (p. lvi): "What
Kant does—stated in broad outline—is to distinguish
between the problems of *existence* and the problems of
value, assigning the former to science and the latter to
philosophy". Before Kant ethical propositions were

thought to be derivable from theoretical (non-ethical)
propositions. The practice of Rationalism was first to
construct a theoretical view of the nature of Reality and
then, by apparently logical inference, to derive an
ethical system from it. Kant set out to show that the
ultimate problems of metaphysics can be solved from
ethical data and from ethical data alone; he succeeded
in showing the self-sufficiency of ethical ideas and their
independence of natural and non-ethical facts.

The immediate importance of this development was
unfortunately clouded in Kant's own work by the
excessive formalism of his ethics, and the Philosophy of
Value as we know it rather took its start in the reaction
from Kant's exaggerated intellectualism. Less direct,
but hardly less important to the development of the
concept of Value, was the revolution in the notion of
personality which he crystallised and largely created.
For the Scholastics, and during the age of Rationalism,
the necessary and sufficient criterion of personality was
rationality, by which was meant the power to recognise
one's own identity through time. Wolff's definition of
personality was as follows: "Persona dicitur ens quod
memoriam sui conservat, hoc est, meminit se esse idem
illud ens quod ante in hoc vel isto fuit statu". This notion
is carried on into the nineteenth century by Herbart's
"Personality is self-consciousness, wherein the ego
regards itself as being one and the same in all its manifold
reactions" (Wke. III, 60). It is not yet extinct. Kant
added the ethical nature as an essential factor in the
notion of personality. In virtue of "animality" man is a
living being; in virtue of "rationality" he is a rational
being; in virtue of "personality" he is autonomous and

responsible. Personality is "that which raises man above himself (as a portion of the sensuous world), that which connects him with an order of things which only reason can think, an order which at the same time has under it the whole sensuous world and with it the empirically-determined existence of man in time and the whole of all purposes" (v, 91, Hart.). By his connection of Freedom and Moral Responsibility with the Pure Practical Reason Kant made not self-consciousness only, but self-consciousness together with self-determination, the necessary and sufficient criterion of personality.

Kant profoundly distrusted the sensuous and passional sides of human nature. He insisted that the apprehension of worth is an act of pure intellectual intuition, in which the emotions play no part. Idealistic theories about Value can trace their origin fairly reasonably from Kant. But psychological theories derive rather from the age immediately subsequent to Kant, and from those aspects in it which were in revolt against the excessive intellectualism of Kant. It was typical of that age to be interested in feeling and will and in those aspects of the psyche in respect of which persons differ. It was engrossed with individuality rather than with the general and universal. Feeling and will are a mode of "rapport" with actuality and they were thought to constitute knowledge of a different aspect of reality from that revealed in theoretical cognition. Their object was said to be *value* or *meaning*. In the early stages the alternatives of subjectivism and objectivism about Value were not envisaged in clear contrast. Feeling is both personal or individual and may be objective in the sense of universal or generally shared. It was thought that in feeling that has universality may be revealed the *concrete nature*, the *meaning*, or the *values* of reality. This sort of view, partaking of the mystical, is typical of what has come to be known as Romanticism.

G. E. Schultze and Jacob Fries, disciples and critics of Kant, both laid great stress on the concept of Value and intimately connected it with feeling. Fries held that apprehension of value consists in feeling and that in feeling we possess a mode of intuitively apprehending the eternal and infinitely Real as it is manifested in the finite and empirical world. The psychological investigation of valuation was carried further by Herbart. Value was connected again more intimately with personality by Lotze and Benecke. They—and in particular Lotze—are not consistent. But the theory which they most generally stand for is the following. The valuable is the proper object of pleasure-pain feeling. Pleasure-pain feeling is an indicator of favourable or harmful influences upon the natural development of personality. Thus "valuableness" is a property of furthering, and "disvalue" of thwarting, the natural development of personality. Benecke writes: "Wir schätzen die Werte aller Dinge nach dem (vorübergehenden oder bleibenden) Steigerungen und Herabstimmungen, welche durch dieselben für unsere psychische Entwicklung bedingt werden".

The course of Value Theory was hereafter carried on chiefly (a) in the Ritschlian school of theology and (b) by the Austrian economists. The modern psychological theories start directly from the epoch-making works of Meinong and von Ehrenfels. The heritage of the confusion inherent in Romanticism has lain heavy upon them. They still lag tardily behind psychology in the realisation that feeling and emotion, though involving "rapport" with an external world of actuality, and directors of theoretical speculation, are not themselves a mode of cognition.

Finally, Realistic theories of Value have arisen more recently from the analogy of Realism in epistemology. They differ from the Kantian tradition in using the analogy of sensation rather than the analogy of immediate intellectual intuition of ultimate truths, to explain the apprehension of Value.

Idealism, or the practical faith in Value, is the proper appanage of the human spirit. I speak not of a philosophical creed, and still less of a predisposition to optimism, but rather of a universal and fundamental psychological motive. The vague and tentative insight by which man pierces beyond the present and "created" to the attainment of a dim and evanescent anticipation of a future stage in his spiritual development guarantees both the content of his aim and the continuance of his endeavour. The darkly visible "not yet" impels in the name of Good or Value, and invests itself with the force of a "must be". In an evolving world the machinery of evolution becomes self-conscious—albeit but gropingly and mistily—at the level of spirit and personality. In the study of man, if it be sufficiently freed from parochiality, we can observe evolution as it were from within. Human progress has been controlled but not directed by the vicissitudes of external environment. Biological needs are always with us, but at no point are they a whole-cause. Their operation is negative. They set the limits and narrow the channel of evolution; but the formative and directing principle lies in human nature itself. It is that radical though volcanic instinct of idealism which impels man to "adapt" himself to something within and yet pointing beyond himself. The urge of the ideal is expressed in the imperative mood. By disobeying external or environmental claims a man may forfeit his life; by disloyalty to the demands of the ideal he must destroy his soul, or in other words his proper humanity. The idealistic impulse is the motive force and steering wheel of progress. It finds its intellectual expression in philosophy, its imaginative and emotional embodiment in religion.

Herein is revealed the fundamental inadequacy of philosophical hedonism. Pleasure is essentially static, clinging to past pleasant experience. It does not contain within itself the seeds of new advance. True happiness has been found by the unanimous experience of all ages to be a by-product of active endeavour in pursuit of a concrete ideal to which the enthusiasm of the whole personality may be harnessed. Pleasure becomes an end in its own right only at those periods of slackness when the impulse to idealism and the possibility of progress are temporarily effete. The dissatisfaction attendant upon idealism is the incentive to progress; contentedness the drag on the evolutionary wheel.

That the ideal—under which term must be subsumed the related concepts of duties and moralities, racial and personal, and the "Ideal Values", which stand in a category apart from all other objects of human endeavour and are held to be incommensurable with them—that this sense of the ideal has been a steady and a powerful directing agency of progress is a plain fact of history which could only be denied by those who, in virtue of behaviouristic or biological preconvictions, are unable to do justice to the psychological existence of ideals. So long as we remain planted upon the firm ground of facts and forbear to theorise about them, it is indubitable that constant attempted pursuit of Value has been the main propulsive force in the development of mankind. But the instinct of idealism is not simply a kind of incoherent clairvoyance of a possible "not yet", carrying with it the unique compulsion of duty. It is sustained by the projection upon the visible world of qualities whose ultimate origin is to be sought in the depths of the human soul. Man is confronted with the vastness and the mystery, with the seeming impermeability to spiritual ideals, of the physical universe. The stirrings of Value within him impel him to postulate a Reality outside himself compensatory at once of his own deficiencies and of the alien nature of his apparent environment. Thus at the very heart of idealism lie that questioning of the apparent and postulation of an ideal Reality, from which both religion and philosophy spring. Philosophy is the quest for certain knowledge of the Reality whose very possibility is first revealed by faith. The diffidence of the individual is unable to support the pregnant idealism of his nature, which irresistibly impels him to belief in a Reality invested with a majesty corresponding to his own weakness, and a holiness for which he longs. Every man is pusillanimous in his own interests: he draws upon the strength of the gods when fighting the cause of the gods. The active idealism in man demands sanction and support from a Reality—religionists say from a personal Reality—transcending individual and society.

It is the faith of religion and the hope of philosophy that this belief is, at its central core, veridical. Philosophy, no less than religion, is projective through and through. No philosopher can *prove* the existence of anything other than his own thought. At most he can prove that the belief in solipsism is for him impossible.

While religion remains essentially faith that the aspiration to "god-likeness" is an effort for rapprochement to a genuine Reality, philosophy undertakes the task of grasping that Reality in thought and substantiating faith by reason. Articulate philosophy emerges from the mythopoeic and collective thought of pre-philosophical ages, which, says M. Robin, "s'accomplit d'une façon impersonnelle, obscure et continue; il accompagne et exprime le mouvement des mœurs et du sentiment religieux".[1] Here the individual contribution is submerged beneath the collective ownership. "La pensée distincte n'est jamais que le dernier anneau d'une longue chaîne de pensées obscures, de besoins et d'actions qui l'ont préparée. Tout commence dans l'inconscient; et s'il est faux de soutenir que l'homme sans la conscience ne serait pas pour cela plus mauvaise machine intellectuelle, il est certain du moins que son apparition est tardive, et qu'elle a, dans ses premiers pas, à recueillir, sous bénéfice d'inventaire, un héritage énorme qu'elle n'a pas accumulé."[2] The new factor which is responsible for the birth of self-conscious philosophy is the spirit of criticism which would substitute rationally grounded knowledge for uncritical acceptance of traditional belief,

[1] "La Pensée Grecque."
[2] A. Lalande, "Revue de Synthèse historique", ii, 205 (quoted by Henri Berr in his Introduction to the above).

would eliminate error, and supplant one-sided dogma by clear vision. Thus philosophy has a double nature—critical and constructive. "As a creed of life philosophy has to meet two needs. Men expect of it a comprehensive, securely based, and, as far as possible, complete structure of all knowledge, and at the same time a definite conviction which will prove a support in life."[2] In different ages and individuals the one or the other of these functions has predominated. Preponderance of the critical attitude, with its fanatical devotion to "certainty" in season and out of season, reduces philosophy to the status of a handmaid to the sciences, and in the last resort to a mere game for those who enjoy intellectual gymnastics for their own sake. Atrophy of the critical impulse leads philosophy back to imaginative and mythopoeic creation. Philosophy has, however, a creative function in harmony with the general impulse of Idealism. "It is one of the permanent aims of philosophy to seek a true Reality behind apparent Reality." Philosophy is the articulate and critical expression of faith in the reality of the ideal, intellectual, ethical and aesthetic. Critical thought alone cannot be creative and cannot lead to new knowledge. It is essentially introspective, being limited to examination and purification of the thought-process itself.

The elaboration of the intellectual ideal (for coherence and applicability, the criteria of theoretical philosophy, are intellectual ideals) has occupied the greater part of the history of philosophy proper. The examination of Value in general, and the ethical and aesthetic values in particular, is the special problem of

[1] Windelband, "Introduction to Philosophy", Engl. trans., p. 27.

philosophy in our own day. It is the business of philosophy to investigate intellectually the instinctive assumption that the sense of Value, which has played and plays
so important a function in the spiritual evolution of
mankind, is a faculty of awareness and does mediate
knowledge of values which are objective to humanity
and integral to the nature of ultimate Reality. The
philosopher must test the intellectual grounds of this
primitive act of faith. When the philosophy of Value
first emerged as distinct from theoretical philosophy it
was assumed, as we have seen, by Kant that we have
immediate intellectual intuition of principles of Right
and Value which form the primordial warp of ultimate
Reality, and by his immediate successors that in certain
feelings we have immediate knowledge, of a non-
theoretical kind, of the ultimate and eternal nature of
Reality, which in sense-perception and theoretical knowledge we know only imperfectly and as it were in
images. The development of psychological theory has
tended to distinguish feeling and emotion sharply from
awareness. And the trend of psychological theory of
Value has been to deny both our knowledge and the
existence of values outside ourselves.

The second problem of the philosopher is to separate
individual, changing and temporary valuations from the
persistent valuations of the race, and secondary and
derived valuations from primary and fundamental valuations. This is, I think, the task of psychology. The
general unsatisfactoriness of psychological theories of
Value has been due to the attempt to solve the former
problem by psychology, a necessarily impossible task.
For psychology is a science, limited to the sphere of

facts, and cannot pronounce upon questions of validity. This second problem, which does belong to psychology, in the widest sense of the word, has as yet been hardly investigated. Its investigation is of course not dependent upon the prior solution of the former problem. Only when the two problems are confused is the result disastrous.

The following pages are devoted solely to the problem of validity. They do not pretend to offer an exhaustive discussion of that problem but to lay down the logical foundations for such a discussion. Still less do they pretend to offer an exhaustive survey of the philosophy of Value. As there are several theories in the field about the nature of valuation and the validity of our sense of Value, the discussion has naturally taken the form of a classification of those theories and examination of their logical bases. It has been the writer's endeavour to give a sound foundation for future work rather than to aspire to specious but precarious originality. He has thought it very unlikely that any theory backed by serious and competent thinkers should be *wholly* wrong and very possible that no essential aspect of the problem has been wholly neglected by so many previous thinkers. Yet it has been necessary to recognise how much the philosophy of Value has suffered from the temporal priority of theoretical philosophy, since even now many, and perhaps most, of its exponents have come to it with habits of mind and predisposition to belief already formed in the field of theoretical metaphysics.

The spiritual ascent of man, alone so far as we know among the evolving strands of the world, is fuliginously illuminated by incipient self-consciousness, a fitful glow from within. We see some little way in advance, in so far as the future stages of the spiritual growth of the race are stirred as ideals to motion within our being. For self-consciousness is the power to look within. We can contemplate in ourselves, and so in others, the process in which we partake. The ideal when recognised compels with the force of an imperative sharply contrasted with the natural force of desires and unidealised impulses. But though a particular ideal when assented to is always imperative, the continued psychological validity of the ideal in general is found to depend, in all but some few outstanding minds of a rationalistic temper, upon a general faith in its harmony with a cosmic Reality transcending the individual and the race as a whole. Religion is the deliberate acceptance of this faith in a cosmic Reality in sympathy with, and including within itself, the ultimate ideals or values of humanity. Philosophy is the justification or refutation of this faith in an intellectual system ruled by the intellectual ideals of coherence and applicability. A complete system of philosophy must therefore be ultimately a philosophy of Value.

FOUNDATIONS OF THE PHILOSOPHY OF VALUE

CHAPTER I

CURRENT THEORIES ABOUT VALUE

THE deplorable *imbroglio* in which the Philosophy of Value is entangled has been to no slight extent due to persistent confusion between problems of Philology and problems of Philosophy. When two men of keen and penetrative intelligence write wisely and well upon two different things, there can be no immediate conflict between their views. For conflicting views must be about the same thing. The selection of the same word by which to refer to the objects of their speculations is insufficient to provide the identity of content from which philosophical disagreement must initiate. But the limitation of sapience to which subtle minds are prone has often accounted for profitless tilting on the field of Philosophy about problems which come only within the province of the grammarian. Current theories about Value are concerned with different things and their only source of contact is the common use of one set of terms, to which they severally ascribe different meanings. Argument between theories thus initially separated cannot advance beyond persuasion, and discussion becomes objurgation. From the habitual presumption that the use of a common set of terms implies a common content of ideas—from the confusion of verbal with conceptual definition—

derives in large part the "trostlos Bild"[1] of Value-
philosophy to-day.

A glance at some of the scattered definitions and
epitaphs upon Value will amply illustrate the maelstrom
of current theories. The science of Value, we are told
by the more conservative, embraces, while at some
points extending, the field of traditional Ethics.[2]
"Value" is synonymous with "good and evil", and to be
preferred because of its freedom from the theological
and transcendental implications of those words in the
older philosophy.[3] More broadly, values are ideals; and
the Absolute Values are the Absolute Ideals of Truth,
Beauty and Goodness. From "ideal" the definitions
advance along the path of generality to "purpose", and
thence to that vague and vagrant word "meaning". With
more definiteness we get a group of "psychological"
definitions. Value is "satisfaction", "desire", "enjoyment", "an attitude taken up towards an object that is
valued". Distinct from such individualistic conceptions
is the group of "social" definitions, falling roughly into
two sub-classes: either, Value is the object of socially
approved ideals or purposes; or, it is conduciveness to
the prosperity of society. Intellectually quite unrelated
to the foregoing are the metaphysical definitions such as
Whitehead's, who finds Value in the concreteness of
actual as opposed to conceptual existence. In another
opposed and unrelated class stand the Realists, who
think Value to be undefinable and unanalysable—a simple

---

[1] The phrase is used by W. Strich, "Das Wertproblem in der Philo-
sophie der Gegenwart".
[2] Sorley, Bosanquet, etc.
[3] J. S. Mackenzie, "Ultimate Values", pp. 15, 93.

and intrinsic quality of things. And, finally, Value has been heralded into the missionary field by theological authors.

Now were we asked soberly to believe that all these presumptive definitions or indications of the nature of Value endeavour to define or to indicate *the same thing* we should be involved in a veritable philosophical nightmare, in which nothing was itself rather than another thing and anything might seem to be anything at all. It is as fantastically irrational to suppose that the same object should be taken by so many observers to be the relation which arises between a desiring person and the object of his desire, social salvation, and a simple unanalysable property, as it would be to suppose that three men confronted with the same object could describe it severally as a quadruped of the genus *equus*, a rack for the drying of clothes, and an instrument of torture. In order to preserve our mental sanity we must accept the obvious conclusion that the "theories about Value" are about different things obscured under the same name. And this conclusion is put beyond reasonable doubt by the consideration that the various writers have not only given different and apparently unconnected definitions of Value, but detect its presence in as widely different fields. If two men looking in opposite directions describe differently the contents of their fields of vision, it is comparatively unimportant that they should both employ the same word to indicate the totality of what they observe.

If this conclusion seem presumptuous or, by ascribing over-much simplicity to subtle minds, seem itself to partake of *naïveté*, we answer that the word "Value" has wide and deeply seated emotional associations, from which philosophers are no more exempt than lesser men. Although emotional considerations should be strictly banished from objective science, they inevitably exert a powerful, and sometimes a decisive, influence over the choice of vocabulary. Hence the philosophers have not been "philosophical" enough to waive the terminology, while insisting upon the content.

CHAPTER II

DEFINITION OF VALUE

THE attempt to construct a philosophy of Value presupposes at least a general intuitive understanding of what Value is. And whether we are engaged in the construction of a philosophical theory of Value or are merely examining existing theories, it is essential to begin by defining what Value means. This is the more necessary because verbal confusion abounds. I say advisedly "what Value *means*" and not "what Value *ought to mean*", because at this stage the latter inquiry could be only verbal and not philosophical.

Definition is of various kinds. The definition of "horse" found in a dictionary should be a compendious statement of the distinctive characteristics of the group or groups of things designated correctly by the word "horse" and should serve as a sufficient guide to the proper use of the word. The definition of the scientist would give us those properties of the *genus* "horse" whereby we might distinguish any member of the *genus* from anything at all not belonging to the *genus*. "Scientific" definition differs from "dictionary" definition in that it is concerned with the discrimination of things and the latter with the correct use of language. It is useful in conducing to greater familiarity with the materials of the world around us but has no immediate implications for philosophy. For it begins and rests in things as they are seen to be. Finally there is "mathematical" or conceptual definition, which is the stuff from which philosophy is made. We first define what we mean by the *idea* "God" and then endeavour to persuade ourselves and others that that idea has a counterpart in existence. We first define the *idea* "democracy" and then exemplify it from existing constitutions. We first define the *idea* "triangle" and then apply it to various approximations in the material of actuality. It is probably true that all conceptual ideas have genetically arisen from the data of sense-perception. But that is irrelevant. For the idea goes beyond perception; and it must be defined in itself and apart from its affinities in perception before it is material for philosophy.

Now the survey in the last chapter precludes the possibility any longer of immediately resorting to conceptual definition in the philosophy of Value. For an application of the principle of "dictionary" definition showed that the rival theories about Value embody different conceptual definitions of different ideas and not different attempts conceptually to define the same idea. The philosophers are not mistaken about the nature of the same thing "Value", but are mistaken in thinking that they are trying to define the same thing; whereas they are successfully defining different things. Hence to add another arbitrary definition would be but to increase existing confusion.

Nor can "dictionary" definition be of any use except in clarifying our starting-point. The word "value" has several meanings in everyday speech. The publisher sets a certain "value" upon Mr Whitehead's *The Aims of Education*; the country schoolmistress affirms that the inspiration which she derives from it has a "value" which cannot be assessed in money; the educational superintendent prognosticates that it will be of "value" in his propaganda for educational reform; and the University don remarks that it contains a "valuable" plea for the recognition of the "Ultimate Values" of Truth and Beauty in education. Here we have "value" used in the spheres of economics, emotion, utility, and tea-party philosophy. But in any case the philosopher, as a specialist, is justified in adopting a word from everyday language into philosophy with a particular and specialised meaning. All we can ask him is to provide, as early as possible in his book, a *dictionary* definition of the word in its special meaning, and not thereafter to resort to any of its accepted everyday usages.

There remains scientific or empirical definition. Although this is not immediately philosophical, it may be possible, by an examination of a wide selection of particular instances of "value", to arrive at a scientific generalisation which will, in its turn, induce a state of apprehension psychologically more apt to give rise to an idea which *may* be conceptually defined.

Proceeding empirically, we should ask ourselves what is the set of characteristics peculiar to all those situations in the description of which we use the word "value" or its cognate terms, and distinguishing them as a class from all those situations to which we do not apply the word. But we should be met at the outset by radical differences of opinion about the relevant data. There is no general agreement about the field of application of "value". Some writers have thought that there is no state of affairs that may not in appropriate circumstances acquire value, or even that there is no state of affairs that is ever entirely neutral in respect of value. Others have held that only states or qualities of human beings, or concrete situations containing such states as constituents, possess value. And there are well-nigh innumerable stages of opinion ranging between these extremes. Moreover all such delimitations of the field of application of "value" presuppose a specific definition of the concept of "Value" because it is impossible to discuss where any word may or may not be appropriately applied by the philosopher, except on the basis of antecedent agreement as to its connotation.

In operation, therefore, the empirical method is at once involved in a dilemma. Either we must distinguish among the actual applications of "value" as right and wrong, philosophically appropriate and inappropriate—and that is to abandon empiricism; or demarcation of the data, and with it empirical definition, is impossible. Philosophers have, in fact, compromised between arbitrary selection among the data and loyalty to the empirical method at the cost of insignificance in the result. Professing to proceed empirically only, they have made use of an unconfessed (and perhaps not consciously realised) conceptual definition as their criterion of relevance in the "empirical" data. Mr Perry has expressly defined the purpose of a "General Theory of Value" to consist in the identification of a common principle underlying all special spheres of Value.[1] By this means the social sciences, theory of knowledge, aesthetics, philosophy of religion, together with the "particular values" of everyday life and social intercourse, are to be "unified and distinguished". His general concept is "biological interest". But Mr Perry has limited his "field of appli-

[1] "General Theory of Value."

cation" to objects standing in relation to animal or human interest and extended it to include all such objects. He takes no consideration of the uses of the word "value" in mathematics, logic, or chemistry, and arbitrarily excludes such philosophical applications as that relation between *any* two existents called by J. Laird (after Francis Bacon) "natural election", or Professor Whitehead's "prehension". Thus his definition is really latent in the selectivity of his data and not derived empirically from his data. Meinong, again, has attempted a philological classification of the applications of "value", in which he includes even its mathematical sense.[1] But the intellectual contortions by which he extracts therefrom a common underlying notion are more interesting as a philosophic curiosity than as a genuine contribution to thought—as, indeed, he himself admits by his immediate return to a more concrete conception of Value. And finally, the "experimental method" (*i.e.* the word-test) was introduced from experimental psychology into the philosophy of Value by Th. Haering.[2] It is superficially obvious that the psychological definition of Value which he professes to have proved experimentally derives either from his own unconscious assumption of that definition in arranging his tests, or from the uncritical verbal habits of his subjects, or from a combination of these factors. It is impossible to *prove* any philosophical doctrine experimentally; and in this case no more could be proved than that "value" is generally associated in the popular mind with interest,

[1] "Zur Grundlegung der allgemeinen Werttheorie."

[2] "Untersuchungen zur Psychologie der Wertung" ("Archiv für die gesamte Psychologie", 1913); cf. W. Gruehne, "Neuere Untersuchungen zum Wertproblem."

desire, pleasure, etc. This no philosopher would deny. It is bad science and bad philosophy to hold an experiment valid of negative results unless it could also have yielded positive results.

The empirical method is open to a further objection. Granted that an empirical definition has been found, and a certain set of characteristics detected to be present in every state of affairs characterised by value: it does not follow that this set of characteristics is identical with the idea of Value. It may be an invariable concomitant of, and yet a different thing from, Value.

CHAPTER III

CLASSIFICATION OF THEORIES ABOUT VALUE

THE results of the precedent chapters may be briefly summarised. First, the definitions of Value sustained in the various theories are sufficiently clear to show that they *must* be attempts to define different things and not discordant attempts to define the same thing. Second, the radical disagreement between various philosophers about the sections of reality in which they find value to exist, or to be capable of existing, supports the view that they envisage different and not the same notions by the word "Value", and also precludes the possibility of arriving at a definition of Value by empirical inspection of existing values. For it shows that Value, unlike beauty or yellow, is not a thing which, although difficult to define conceptually, is understood intuitively so that it can be recognised with comparative certainty by men who are confronted with it.

The problem now before us is the source of the controversy between exponents of the various theories about Value. In so far as men are writing about different things they do not as a rule find it necessary to enter into discussion with a view to invalidating each other's opinions. A practical economist writing on "Valuation" would have no interest in attacking Professor Urban. But philosophers writing upon Value, although they have meant things as different by "Value" as did Professor Urban and the practical economist, have thought themselves obliged to discredit "conflicting" theories. We have, then, to look for connection; for there can be no conflict without connection.

Theories of Value carry with them immediate implications about the nature of Reality. They are, indeed, primarily asseverations about the nature, or an aspect of the nature, of Reality. This is the point of contact. It has proved unfortunate that Philosophy of Value as a distinct field of speculation emerged late in the history of thought and after the main attitudes in metaphysics and epistemology had been already differentiated. Value has tended to become infected with a large part of the emotional influence which his own beliefs about Reality exercise upon the mind of every philosopher. In illustration of this it may be noticed that philosophers have tended to introduce Value at a point in their theories which is distinctive of their attitudes towards Reality. Professor Whitehead has used it at the point of contact between the conceptual and the actual; Mr Perry finds it to be co-extensive with "biological interest"; Professor Alexander has connected it with the "emergence" of new levels of being. And so on.

Theories about Value meet, then, first upon the level of *Weltanschauung* or general theory about Reality, and the controversy cannot be settled immediately by examination and comparison of arguments about the definition or location of value. In the present state of the matter it would be both rash and presumptuous to advance new personal opinions about Value. And the various theories have been adequately stated and intelligently, if acrimoniously, attacked and defended. The first requisite of solid advance is to classify the types of theory which are offered and to inspect their foundations and implications. The basis of classification must be their bearing upon *Weltanschauung*.

CHAPTER IV

NATURALISTIC AND NON-NATURALISTIC THEORIES

IF the principle of classification of theories about
Value is to be their essential implications for *Weltan-schauung* or general theory about Reality, we must
commence from Dr Broad's bifurcation of ethical
theories into naturalistic and non-naturalistic theories.
In his own words, "The first and most fundamental
problem of pure ethics is whether these characteristics
are unique and peculiar, in the sense that they cannot
be analysed *without remainder* in terms of non-ethical
characteristics. . . . Those theories which hold that ethical
characteristics *can* be analysed without remainder into
non-ethical ones may be called *Naturalistic Theories*; those
which hold that they cannot may be called *Non-Naturalistic Theories*".[1] For Value Philosophy the problem
is whether by "Value" we denote a concept which is
unique and *sui generis*, or whether we do not.

Professor A. E. Taylor has objected to the importance
assigned to this distinction on the ground that it may
become ambiguous in application.[2] Both Plato and
Spinoza would assent to the definition of virtue as the
efficient performance of the "activities of the species to
which you belong". And nevertheless Spinoza should,
and Plato could not, be classed as a "naturalist" in
respect of Value, if the distinction between "naturalist"
and "non-naturalist" is to retain any significance at all.

---

[1] "Five Types of Ethical Theory", p. 257.
[2] Review of the above in "Mind".

The ambiguity, however, lies not in Dr Broad's distinction but in the definition of virtue, which in Spinoza's case is meant to be understood biologically, and when used by Plato would imply reference to a non-analysable ideal of good. They understand different things by "proper activities of the species". No principle of classification can hope to rise superior to the ambiguities in the definitions which it is intended to classify. And in classifying one must be perpetually on the alert for such ambiguities.

To state the distinction between naturalistic and non-naturalistic in more general language: We may think of the totality of existence as consisting of a number of simple qualities not built up out of others and of compound qualities which are combinations of simple qualities. Colours are simple qualities. We say that orange is composed of red and yellow, meaning that when we mix red and yellow pigments in certain proportion we produce orange pigment. But however often we look at a primrose and a carnation we shall not obtain the sensation which we achieve by looking at a marigold. The *sense-quality* orange is simple and un-analysable. Now we will exclude from the total content of existence that quality, whatever it is, which we mean by "Value". Can the whole of existence then be completely described by mentioning those simple qualities which are left and their combinations? The naturalist about Value says it can; the non-naturalist says that such a description would omit one simple quality which exists. The practical importance of the quality in question renders the difference of paramount importance for our metaphysical conception of Reality. It is not merely a question whether a quality which is apprehended by all and admitted to exist by all is simple or complex—as we might discuss whether orange is simple or analysable. The non-naturalists perfectly understand the complex combination of qualities which the naturalists call "Value"; but they assert that *another* quality exists, which is not that combination and which they call "Value". The naturalists deny that that quality does exist.

If the naturalists are right, it follows that the non-naturalists are talking about an *Unding*—something which really does not exist at all, but which they have mistakenly supposed to exist. "Value" is in their mouths a meaningless term, their value-theories simply emotive noise. If, on the other hand, the non-naturalists can justify their contention, the naturalists have failed to detect a particularly important characteristic of Reality and have constructed their theories as though no such characteristic existed. Either they are convicted of axiological colour-blindness, as it were, or the non-naturalists are the subjects of a peculiarly virulent delusion which unfits them for the task of metaphysics. This is the essential meeting-point around which debate should centre, and apart from it *the two types of theory have no point of contact.*

The issue between naturalism and non-naturalism must be faced directly and has usually been shirked. As an example of the *wrong* method of approach may be adduced Professor Urban's *Valuation, its Nature and its Laws.* "Value" is asserted to be the property of being an object of the non-cognitive mental act which he calls "valuation". The book contains a profound and intricate psychological explanation of the ramifications and development of "valuation". If his initial conception of the nature of Value is right, his theory about Value is all that could be desired, and the non-naturalists are in fact deluded. If, however, they have discovered, and are calling attention to, a real characteristic of things, then Professor Urban's theory remains good psychology; but his metaphysics of Reality resulting therefrom would be flagrantly fallacious, because it would neglect the important aspect of Reality with which the philosophy of Value should be concerned. And hardly the most desultory attempt is made to show that this is not the case. Once a definition of Value has been assumed, there is no way of justifying the assumption by elaboration from it and no way of proving it by the consequences which may be adduced. Every writer is bound by his initial definition. Professor Sorley is completely justified in his protest against the philosophical hustling in which naturalists are fain to indulge: "The method of psychological inquiry is misconceived, and its results are misinterpreted when these are allowed to take the place of an independent investigation of value. The experiences and judgement of value are undoubtedly mental facts, and psychology may trace their rise and history; but it does not touch the question of their validity, any more than the question of the validity of mathematical judgements is affected by the history of their formation".[1] Unless, therefore, the issue between naturalistic and non-naturalistic theories has already been decided, the elaboration of the consequences of a theory belonging to either class runs the risk of being proved to be irrelevant—non-naturalistic theories of being mere word-play

[1] "Moral Value and the Idea of God."

and about nonentities, and naturalistic theories of talking about facts which might equally well be described without having recourse to the terminology of Value, while neglecting the realities with which the philosophy of Value has to do.

As many of the less careful or less honest writers have the habit of introducing a definition of Value implicitly into their presuppositions before allowing it overtly to intrude into the argument, it has been easy for the protagonists on both sides to give to their conclusions something of the factitious obviousness of the truism. The naturalists tend to describe circles with the inevitability of children on the roundabouts. The non-naturalist, preferring the swings, indulges in recapitulated assurance, hoping to gain by importunity that which he is unable to prove by reason.

The naturalist has to prove that the concept of Value *sui generis*—a simple and not analysable quality—is an unwarrantable inference from the structure of language, or else that it derives from antecedent metaphysical presuppositions and analogies, which are false. Practical thinking, it is well known, tends to identify personal conviction with objective validity; and language is incurably objective. The suggestion is, that certain philosophers have been systematically trained to mistake the grammar of language for the grammar of Reality.[1] It cannot, indeed, be well denied that the great majority of the value-judgements in common speech are simply records of personal and private reactions to objective situations. Only in form do they postulate the existence of an objective quality Value. Arguments of this sort

[1] See Ogden and Richards, "The Meaning of Meaning".

carry a great force of persuasion mainly to those who are already convinced that the non-naturalists' belief about Value is wrong; but they do not attack their belief directly. That belief is perfectly consistent with the recognition that what is asserted in these arguments is true. It might even be considered preposterous in the naturalists to discourse upon the sources of delusion of a belief which they have not yet shown to be delusory.

Some non-naturalists, in turn, have professed to think that naturalistic theories depend upon a rather elementary logical confusion between the following two propositions: "(*a*) The ethical characteristic E *synthetically entails and is entailed by* the non-ethical characteristics N_1, N_2, ...; and (*b*) The ethical characteristic E is *analysable without remainder into* the conjunction of the non-ethical characteristics N_1, N_2, ...".[1] McTaggart has written: "It is generally admitted that it is impossible to define good and evil in terms of anything else. Any assertions that this is possible are due, I think, to a confusion between definition and a universal synthetic proposition about the thing defined".[2] The naturalistic position has often been confusedly stated; again, it has been professed by writers who have used expressions and propounded views inconsistent with a naturalistic theory of ethics. But there is no *logical* confusion inherent in the naturalistic position as such. The definition of Value, for instance, (or, for that matter, of good) as "the property of being an object of desire" may imply failure to perceive an aspect of Reality (that has to be argued), but it is not in itself logically ambiguous. The

[1] Broad, op. cit. p. 238.
[2] "The Nature of Existence", ii, 398.

non-naturalists assert that there are two qualities: V, which is simple and unanalysable; and W, which is analysable into the conjuction of the non-Value charac-teristics N_1, N_2, ... These qualities stand to one another in the relation of mutual implication; each is entailed by the other. They further assert that the non-naturalists, falling into a common logical error, suppose themselves to be defining V when they are defining W. This may be true of particular exponents of the naturalistic position, but it is not a valid objection to the position itself. And even if *all* its exponents were liable to this criticism, naturalism itself would not be damaged. For naturalism asserts that there is only *one* quality, and that this is analysable without remainder into the conjunction of the non-Value characteristics N_1, N_2, ...; that there is no V which is not W or W which is not V. They may be mistaken. But if so their mistake is one of intuitive apperception and not one of logic. The attempt on the part of non-naturalists to represent what is a disagree-ment at the level of *intuition* as a *logical* confusion in the minds of their opponents is neither kind nor profitable.

The first and most fundamental problem in the philosophy of Value is, then, to decide between naturalistic and non-naturalistic theories. That issue is metaphysical and must be faced directly. The derivation of a definition of Value from data which implicitly contain that definition adds nothing to its cogency. And the productions of sound reasons why writers on the opposite side *may* be mistaken is no proof that they *are* mistaken.

CHAPTER V

IDEALISTIC THEORIES

THE classification of theories about Value into naturalistic and non-naturalistic is such that every theory must fall into one class or the other. The many subdivisions of naturalism are of minor philosophical importance. The naturalist could describe the totality of existence without having recourse to Value; and his use of Value is to some degree a matter of terminological convenience. In general he uses it to express and emphasise his antecedent attitude towards the empirical world. A thinker of behaviouristic tendency will define it as a biological principle and then extend that principle to include all professed instances of valuation, thus calling attention to his conviction of the continuity or identity, as the case may be, between the psychological and biological realms. One who is convinced of the uniqueness or importance of consciousness (or human consciousness, or the social factor in human consciousness), while admitting genetic continuity, will emphasise his conviction by limiting his use of value-terminology in the appropriate way. In a word, philosophers have introduced Value at that point in their systems which seemed to them to have particular significance and to be in need of a certain emotional underlining.

Non-naturalistic theories, on the other hand, divide into two main classes on an issue of definite metaphysical importance. While both classes hold Value to be a non-natural and unanalysable quality, the one holds it to be a pure, and the other a relational, quality. In order to avoid the cacophonous jargon of "Relational" and "non-Relational Non-Naturalistic Theories", I propose to call the former "Idealistic" and the latter "Realistic" theories about Value.

Realistic theories, then, hold that Value is a non-natural and pure property of natural and existing states of affairs. The significance of "pure non-natural quality" is explained with unusual lucidity and precision by Professor G. E. Moore in his essay "The Conception of Intrinsic Value", which is printed in *Philosophical Studies*. Value is a pure and non-relational property, the specific value of any state of affairs depending solely and entirely upon the intrinsic properties of that state of affairs and not upon any relation in which it may stand to anything else in the universe. But though the value of anything is in fact determined by its intrinsic properties and by these alone, value differs from other intrinsic properties in being logically separable from the state of affairs in which it inheres, without destruction to the identity of that state of affairs. The realist also holds that from the values of things derives a normative relation between them and moral agents, in virtue of which any moral agent *ought* always to act in such a way as to produce a valuable rather than a non-valuable and a more valuable rather than a less valuable state of affairs by his actions. There has been some confusedness in the statements of the connection between *value* and *ought*. Professor Moore has stated that *value* and *oughtness to exist* are terms which connote the same idea and may be used interchangeably. Waiving the question whether "oughtness to exist" should not imply a *relational* property (and so be inconsistent with the *pure* quality value), it is clear that "oughtness to exist" is not identical with the *moral* "ought". For the latter is, and the former is not, in itself a relation one of the terms of which is necessarily a moral agent. It is still more clear that the moral "ought" is not identical with the quality "value". The former is, and the latter is not, a relational property. Hence the Realists postulate *two* ultimate and irreducible concepts, "Value" (non-relational) and "ought" (relational). In order to effect a working connection between Value and the rest of existence they then further affirm that (moral) *oughtness* is synthetically entailed by *Value*.

Idealist theories, on the other hand, acknowledge only one ultimate concept "oughtness", in terms of which *Value* is defined. "Oughtness" is an absolute and underived factor in the structure of Reality, in virtue of which it is said that some things are "more fitting" to exist, or "ought rather" to exist, than others. When we say this we *mean* that where their existence at all depends upon the voluntary action of a moral being he is morally obliged to act in such a way as will further the existence of that thing which is "most fitting" or "ought most" to exist. When a thing is said to be *valuable*, that means simply that it *ought* to be valued or actively desired to exist by moral beings. Thus there is only one non-natural quality, "moral obligation", which is a nonnatural relation between moral beings and the rest of existence. Regarding this as a relational property of things, we speak for convenience of their value or "oughtness to exist".

The distinctness of Idealistic from Realistic theories

should be as apparent as it is important. In the one case Value is defined; in the other it is ultimate and undefinable. Idealistic theory acknowledges only one ultimate notion in Value Philosophy; Realists need two ultimates, neither definable in terms of the other. They are as different in their general philosophical attitudes. Realism tends to picture the universe discretely as a manifold of scattered existents each with its own index of value; it has no disposition towards anthropocentrism. In Idealism mankind, as moral agents, are central; the moral "ought" tends to become regulative not only for man but for the universe. Idealism, too, encourages a unifying rather than a separating outlook upon Reality. No state of affairs can be conceptually isolated and assigned an index of value in virtue of its own intrinsic qualities alone. As valuableness entails relation to the volitional activity of moral agents, so the specific value of any state of affairs can only be stated in comparison with that of all other states of affairs. In every concrete situation involving a moral agent and a state of affairs capable of being influenced by the voluntary actions of the moral agent, the *value* of that state of affairs can only be stated (because his moral obligation towards it can only be stated) in terms of its relation to the value of all other possible states of affairs which could be influenced to exist or not to exist by the voluntary activity of that moral agent at that moment. Actual statements of value are for the most part implied generalisations. A thing is said to be Absolutely valuable when its existence ought in all circumstances to be actively desired by every moral being.

CHAPTER VI

LINGUISTIC CONFUSIONS

BASING our analysis upon ontological differences, and leaving upon one side questions of epistemology and philology, we have discovered three main types of theories about Value. They are Naturalistic and Non-Naturalistic, the latter subdividing into Realistic and Idealistic (Non-Relational and Relational) theories. We have argued that as these ontological issues are of fundamental importance in general metaphysics, so they must occupy the attention of Value-Philosophy explicitly and consciously. Only upon this fundamental level can different types of theory about Value find any common ground upon which to exchange arguments. Once conflicting definitions of Value have been accepted or assumed by two philosophers, they are henceforth debarred from exchanging anything more important in this field than insults or witticisms.

To each theory about Value two criteria must be applied. First, can it be both logically propounded and developed coherently? And second, do the data upon which it is based and the conclusions which may be derived from it conform to observed actuality? But before we proceed to a particular inspection of the various types of theory there remain several verbal confusions to be cleared up.

I. The somewhat haphazard employment of the terms "subjective" and "objective" has been a source of muddled thinking and an impediment to communication as well in philosophy of Value as elsewhere. These words now bear in philosophy meanings the opposite of those with which they were first used by the Scholastics. When "subjective" and "objective" are mutually exclusive and collectively exhaustive alternatives, "subjective" means now what "objective" meant then and "objective" means now what "subjective" meant then. "Subjective" was first used technically by Erigena of the subject-matter of the judgement, the *conceptum*, or (as we should now say) the *object* of thought. "Objective" referred to the *conceptum* in its relation (*objicere*) to thought-processes, and not as independently real. This usage was still frequent in Descartes and is found in Berkeley (Fraser, II, p. 477). The modern usage started with Wolff. It was adopted from him by Kant and became general. "Subjective" now involves relation and "objective" self-subsistence.

But the contrast between "subjective" and "objective" is made both from an epistemological and a psychological point of view. In EPISTEMOLOGY anything that is discovered by or presented to the Self (*Vorgefundensein vom Ich*) is psychologically *objective* but *epistemologically subjective*. Psychological objectivity is the property of standing over against the Self when it is perceiving, thinking, etc. Epistemological objectivity means reality which is independent of the Self and mental processes. The contrast between epistemological objectivity and psychological objectivity (epistemological subjectivity) is roughly that between self-subsistence and existence in relation to mental processes.

PSYCHOLOGY distinguishes three kinds of objectivity. (a) The psychological objectivity of my private perceptual environment (which stands over against and is presented to my Self). The subjective opposite is mind-process—imagination, thinking, etc. (b) The epistemological objectivity of the over-individual or conceptualised world of "common objects". The subjective opposite is private and individual. (c) The absolute reality of noumenal reality. To this corresponds epistemological subjectivity (psychological objectivity) in the epistemologist's sense.

In certain semi-philosophical writings "objective" has a different meaning from any of the above. When Heinroth described Goethe's thought as "objective" he meant that it expresses the general tendencies of the human mind as such. In this application "objective" means "pertaining to the universal constitution of mind or spirit as such" (für alle Denkfähigen notwendig) as opposed to individual idiosyncrasy and difference.

Thus whenever the word "objective" is used the point of view from which the contrast between objective and subjective is envisaged should be made clear. To every meaning for "objective" there is a corresponding meaning for "subjective", and vice versa.

Theories about Value may be classified as objective or subjective. Epistemologically objective (from the point of view of epistemology) are realistic theories, idealistic theories (because moral obligation is independent of the attitude of the moral agent, as moral agent, towards the state of affairs to which he is morally obliged), and those naturalistic theories which define Value independently of a valuer ("Value is utility, e.g. for the permanence of society"; "Value is prehension" etc.).

But within subjective theories about Value objective and subjective values are distinguished on two grounds.

(1) *Generality.* Propositions of the form "X is valuable for me" are said to be subjective. Propositions of the form "X is valuable for such and such a class of persons" are said to be about objective value. They become interesting when they take the form "X is valuable for all normal persons". Further, it may be possible to say "it pertains to the constitution of mind as such—or belongs to the notion of human being—to value X". The objectivity then implied is analogous to the sort of objectivity which Heinroth asserted was possessed by Goethe's thought. Finally, some people have thought that the development of culture and the creation and improvement of empirical values is the progressive manifestation or actualisation in history of the nature of an Absolute and Eternal Spirit. Absolute Value is constituted by the qualities and attributes of the Absolute Spirit. "In reality", writes Eucken, "all historical and social spirituality is only the development of a timeless spiritual life, superior to all mere human existence." Here naturalistic theory merges into non-naturalistic.

(2) *Normative Objectivity.* Certain forms of valuation (*e.g.* the religious) are only possible for a subject who believes that the imaginal construct or conceptual entity valued exists in its own right and is not mind-dependent or created. Such valuational attitudes are conditioned by antecedent appreciative processes of the individual and the race. They exercise a control over incidental individual desires and conations in virtue of a feeling of obligation. The normative objectivity recognised by those who hold (epistemologically) subjective theories about value must not be confused with that postulated by Idealism. The former is dependent upon and causally

conditioned by precedent psychical processes; the latter is logically antecedent to and independent of psychical processes.

Objective in general is the negation of subjective. But it is very important to distinguish between the application of these terms *within* a particular theory about Value and their application to Value theories in order to discriminate between types of definition of Value. To the epistemologist *all* the values postulated in a subjective theory about Value are subjective; but the subjectivist (having once epistemologically defined Value) may, from the standpoint of his theory, discriminate subjective and objective values. Therefore it is essential when one is using these terms to state clearly whether it is from the general epistemological standpoint or from the standpoint of a particular theory.

A special confusion has been introduced by certain writers who, holding that value is constituted by valuation, use "valuation" and "value-judgement" interchangeably. They then assume that subjective theories maintain that value is existentially dependent upon the value-judgement and educe as a facile linguistic refutation of subjective theories that value-judgements must always be true or false. This is mistaken and absurd. Whether they belong to subjective or objective theories about Value, all particular value-judgements are about perfectly determinate and therefore objective facts. The judgement about value must be clearly distinct from the psychical act which psychological theories about Value hold to constitute valuableness. R. B. Perry, for instance, says: "A proposition about value is independent of its being judged". And Dr F. R.

Tennant: "In ethics, as in physics, all significant propositions must be either true or false". The confusion here displayed was originated among the earlier members of the Ritschlian school.

II. A second verbal confusion is, if anything, yet more pervasive, and although it sounds simple in the bald statement may, when practically utilised by a determined exponent, leave his reader crushed and confounded by the sheer impossibility of interpreting his actual beliefs. This is the use of the plural "values" with bewildering dexterity to mean objects of value (*Wertgegenstände*), spheres of existence in which value is found, and determinate qualities under a determinable, "Value", (as *red* and *yellow* are determinate qualities under the determinable *colour*). For instance, Truth, Beauty and Goodness are spoken of as Absolute Values. But while the apprehension of truth, the appreciation of beauty, and the performance of goodness are concrete states of affairs and may be *qualified* by Value; Beauty, Truth and Goodness are abstracts and cannot be qualified by Value. Nor can they be *kinds* of Value. For it is quite impossible to conceive a higher determinable quality under which they can be subordinated. The analogy "Colour—colours" and "Value—values" is linguistic only and corresponds to no possible conceptual content. Whenever confusion might arise it is advisable to use "valuableness" for the quality Value conceived as present to a definite existent, "valued-object" or "value-object" for the existent qualified by Value, and "Value" for the quality when conceived in the abstract.

This confusion seems to pervade those theories which endeavour to combine naturalistic and idealistic conceptions of Value. I follow Reischle, a particularly clear exponent of the type.[1]

The simplest form of value-judgement, he says, asserts an actual or potential relation of the value-object to the valuing person. The type of such value-judgements is "this is valuable (has value) for me". Any object which is believed or supposed to be actual may be valued—may therefore be actually valuable. ("Der Wertung kann irgend welcher in der Vorstellung fixierte Gegenstand unterzogen werden, mögen wir nun von seiner Wirklichkeit überzeugt sein oder ihn hypothetisch als wirklich setzen", p. 27.) The value-relation is described as *satisfaction* (*Befriedigung*) either (in the more elementary forms of valuation) of affective-conational response, or (in more complex value-judgements) of the whole personality (*Befriedigung für mein Gesamt-Ich-Gefühl*). The initial conception of Value is purely naturalistic. It is possible, however, in virtue of the solidarity of human interests to advance beyond the individualistic value-judgement. Not only can I say "X is valuable for me", but "X is valuable for us" or "X is valuable for such and such a class of people". The extension from the "individual" to the "collective" value-judgement is made possible by our power to enter into and understand the interests and valuations of others.[2] To this class belong "economic" values. Such general or collective value-judgements may have partial (*bedingt*) or universal (*unbedingt*) application.

---

[1] "Werturteile und Glaubensurteile."

[2] "Möglich ist uns diese Erfahrung nur auf Grund der Fähigkeit, uns in das Wollen und Fühlen von anderen, auch von denen, mit denen wir in einem Interessenstreit stehen, hinein zu versetzen oder es hypothetisch nachzuerleben." p. 52. Compare von Ehrenfels, "System der Werttheorie", i, 93 ff.

They may be true of a determinate class of men or of all men. But even when of universal truth these value-judgements remain naturalistic. They are empirical generalisations from observed facts. They have *de facto* generality (*Allgemeinheit*) but not necessary, *a priori*, validity (*Allgemeingültigkeit*).

In addition to and distinct from universal natural value-judgements he postulates ideal or normative value-judgements. These assert not that the value-object is valuable for this or that individual or group but that it is in itself valuable. The assertion is made in virtue of an *idea* or *norm*. The validity of the judgement does not depend upon an empirical universality of valuation but upon the intrinsic valuableness of the object; not upon its *actual* valuation but upon its *claim* to be valued. The actual valuations of all persons who value it *ought* to agree with the real value it possesses. ("Wenn wir ein Werturteil als richtig aufstellen, so behaupten wir damit nicht, dass etliche oder viele oder alle thatsächliche so urteilen, sondern wir stellen die Forderung auf, dass alle so urteilen sollen. Diese Forderung aber wäre Brutalität, wenn sie nur bedeutete, dass die andern sich mit ihrer subjektiven Gefühlsweise der unsrigen anschliessen sollten. Ein höheres Recht gewinnt sie nur dann, wenn wir bei unserem Werturteile von dem Bewusstsein eine *Idee oder Norm* geleitet sind, die wir aus innern Gründen anerkennen und deren Verständnis wir auch von andern erwarten können. Da erst tritt an Stelle der empirischen Allgemeinheit von Wertungen und Werturteilen deren Allgemeingiltigkeit", p. 60.) The Norms of ideal value are the ideas of Beauty, Goodness, Truth and Holiness.

The objection here is to the impression conveyed that

there is some connection between the naturalistic and the idealistic parts of the theory. There is none. "Naturalistic value" and "ideal value" are not determinates under a superordinated determinable, Value. The idea of an absolute and *a priori* norm, in virtue of which certain things *ought* to be valued, belongs to a different sphere of thought from the psychology of collective emotion and desire. Ideal valuation is right or wrong; natural valuation is simply fact. It is impossible to reduce natural and ideal value to a single concept, because "naturalistic" and "non-naturalistic" are mutually exclusive. Hence the employment of "value" for both ideas is an unwarrantable perversion of language. It serves no useful purpose, but invites confusion and is logically abhorrent.

III. The contrast between "instrumental" and "intrinsic" value has already been objected to, though I think on improper grounds, by John Laird. For one who holds a naturalistic theory about Value there is, of course, no such thing as "intrinsic value" as that is defined by Professor G. E. Moore in *Philosophical Studies*. For the naturalist all valuableness depends upon the attitude of a valuing subject towards the object valued and nothing is valuable in respect of its own intrinsic properties alone without reference to the attitude of a valuing subject towards it. Hence the naturalist's use of "intrinsic value" must not be confused with the realist's use. Certain things, as for example kindness or a work of art, are valued for themselves alone. Other things, as for example a surgical operation, are valued only in virtue of certain external results which they are the means or instruments for producing. The naturalist calls the former intrinsically and the latter instrumentally valuable.

But if the value-judgement affirms a non-natural property, "instrumental value" is an absurd misnomer. Something which is conducive to the coming into existence of valuable situations may also be valuable in its own right; but its "conduciveness" or instrumentality is not a separate *species* of valuableness. Nor do we call money "instrumentally pleasant" because it is instrumental to the acquisition of pleasure. The realist may point out that a thing is instrumental *in* a state of affairs that is valuable as a totality. But if it has value at all it is intrinsically valuable. On the other hand, the transference of emotion, from the object upon which it was originally directed to something that is instrumental for the acquisition of that object, is a well-known psychological happening. Hence those who hold a psychological theory about the nature of Value may more reasonably speak of "instrumental value". They will mean, when they say that something is instrumentally valuable, that it awakes a feeling of affection or desire *through the knowledge that* it is an instrument for the possession of another thing which is already desired. But in so far as the thing said to be instrumentally valuable does actually arouse affection or desire towards itself, it is also *intrinsically* valuable. But even those who hold psychological theories about Value should distinguish between something which, like wealth, does actually arouse desire through the knowledge that it is an instrument for the possession of things which are desired in themselves, and something which, like a surgical operation, is known to be instrumental towards a state of affairs that is desired but does not (as a rule) awaken feelings of affection or desire.

Laird, speaking from a Realistic position, objects to the distinction between "intrinsic" and "instrumental" value on the following grounds. "When anything is a means or an instrument towards that which is good, there are two alternatives. In the first of these the instrument is not good at all, although it has good effects; in the second the instrument acquires a virtue which it would not have if it were idle, or employed for some other purpose. If it does acquire this virtue, it does acquire it; and therefore it *is* good as long as it is effectively employed in this fashion. The genuine distinction, in short, is between things which are good in certain employments *only*, and things which are either always good and in all employments, or at any rate are good in some other fashion than simply in this limited one."[1] For the idea of "intrinsic" good he would substitute the idea of "dominating" good, and by this expression he understands something which is in all circumstances good as to its consequences and influences. "What we seek, in a word, is not something which ' would be good quite alone ',[2] but a dominant good—one which, irradiating its surroundings, dignifies whatever it touches. Such a good might or might not be good 'quite alone'. If it is a dominating good, its intrinsic goodness matters very little."

Now this will not do. In the first place, the idea of "dominant" good logically presupposes that of intrinsic good. For it is impossible to decide whether something

---

[1] "A Study in Moral Theory", p. 44.
[2] Professor G. E. Moore's phrase.

has or has not good consequences unless it be in virtue of the intrinsic goodness, or lack of intrinsic goodness, of its consequences. But more important (because Laird does not deny intrinsic value, although he belittles its importance), it presupposes a *psychological* conception of causality which is inconsistent with its postulation of objective value in virtue of causation. Psychologically we regard the surgical operation as the *cause* of our health and may look back upon it with feelings of affection; but actually it is only one element in the cause. Other elements are the continuation of the solar system, the continued presence of oxygen in the earth's atmosphere, the condition of the body upon which the operation was performed, etc. There is nothing that is causally unrelated in the universe. The cause of any state of affairs is the total state of the rest of the universe. Faithfulness to this (objective) notion of causality would mean that it was impossible to distinguish between good and bad in virtue of consequences. For the causes of any state of affairs which was intrinsically good would include, among the rest of the universe, things which were bad. But it is grossly confusing to postulate (epistemologically) objective value in virtue of a *psychological* notion of causality. I am inclined to believe, and should like to suggest, that Professor Laird's conception of "dominant" causality has its origin in a naïve hypostatisation from the psychology of emotion and desire.

IV. One final confusion remains to be cleared up. Many philosophers who have approached ethics empirically have become more interested in the discovery of a reliable criterion of good and bad than in the analytical definition of goodness. When Hume wrote, "Whatever is valuable in any kind, so naturally classes itself under the division of *useful* or *agreeable*, the *utile* or the *dulce*, that it is not easy to imagine, why we should ever seek further, or consider the question as a matter of nice research or inquiry";[1] he was proposing such a criterion. He himself thought that value should be analytically defined as 'the property of being an object of a unique and peculiar emotion', which he called the "moral sentiment". All writers have not been so clear as Hume and many have confused a criterion or universal concomitant of value with an analytical definition of value. It is necessary to make clear whether one is proposing a criterion whereby valuable objects may be easily distinguished from non-valuable objects or propounding an analytical definition of the quality Value.

[1] "An Inquiry concerning the Principles of Morals."

CHAPTER VII

SUBJECTIVE THEORIES (a) PSYCHOLOGICAL

BY Subjective Theories about Value I shall mean those theories which define Value in relation to non-cognitive mental states. They differ from Realistic theories, which do not define Value; from Idealistic theories, which define it in relation to an absolute non-natural relation to moral agents; and from such non-natural theories as define it as a relation one of the terms of which is not necessarily psychical.

According to subjective theories "valuable" is a diadic or relational adjective.[1] Like "amiable", its function is to *relate* two substantives. Significant propositions about valuableness are incurably of the form "X has value for Y". "Every value", says Meinong, "must be value for a subject."[2] And von Ehrenfels: "Each single value exists only for a subject—strictly speaking, for a definite subject at a definite time".[3] Propositions of the form "X has value" are strictly indeterminate until a definite class of valuers for whom X has value is understood.

Realistic theories hold that the grammatical structure of value-judgements in ordinary speech is a logically correct emblem of the proposition meant to be asserted in them. Subjective theories, on the other hand, divorce the real and the grammatical content of value-judgements. Dr F. R. Tennant says: "That a value-judgement,

[1] Cf. Johnson, "Logic", Part I, chap. xiii.
[2] "Psychologische-ethische Untersuchungen zur Werttheorie", p. 27.
[3] "System d. Werttheorie", i, 66.

such as 'that act is noble' has grammatically the same form as the judgement 'the sky is blue', disguises its nature: linguistically convenient, and practically harmless, it is philosophically inaccurate or superficial".[1] Meinong, in direct contradiction, says: "The heavens are called beautiful in no other sense than that in which they are called blue".[2]

At this level three types of value are distinguished, actual, dispositional, and potential. *Actual* value is constituted by actual and experienced (*erlebt*) emotional attitude towards an object. My friend has actual value for me when I am actually feeling affection for him. But his value for me is not entirely dependent upon the vagaries of my emotional attitudes; there is a sense in which it is constant and remains even when he is absent from my thoughts. I have a constant disposition to be distressed at his sufferings, to rejoice in his presence, to feel sadness at the idea of possible estrangement, and so forth. I should be willing to undergo a certain amount of personal discomfort in order to help him. The object of a relatively constant emotional and conative disposition is said to have *dispositional* value. Finally, an object may have neither actual nor dispositional value, but may be judged to be likely to acquire actual or dispositional value in circumstances which it is reasonable to suppose are likely to occur. Thus children are told that the acquirement of learning or the building up of methodical habits will be valuable to them in the future. In such cases the object is said to have *potential* value. Propo-

[1] "Philosophical Theology", i, 156–7.
[2] Quoted by W. R. Sorley in "Moral Values and the Idea of God", p. 77. (In his later writings Meinong had abandoned the subjective theory.)

sitions about potential value should strictly take the form "X would have value for Y in Z-like circumstances". They are often confused with propositions about *utility*. But the two are not the same. For I need not necessarily ever value what I or others judge to be useful for me. It is possible to make a consistent habit of veracity from the conviction that it is useful, without ever acquiring a feeling of affection for veracity in oneself.

The elementary "definitions" of Value with which most psychological theories start (*e.g.* valuableness = desiredness) should be regarded as emblems of the logical nature of the theory intended to be maintained rather than true definitions which are to be consistently upheld. They are concrete illustrations of the more general proposition "Value is relation to non-cognitive mental states". The development of the theory should be guided by two aims, (a) to render the general logical definition of Value given above more definite, by analysing and specifying the "non-cognitive mental states"; and (b) to show that that definition comprises all genuine instances of value. The problem with which all psychological theories must cope is to bring within the scope of this general definition of Value the "higher" stages of valuation which are acknowledged to exist in ethics, aesthetics, etc. At these higher levels the value-judgement seems to assert more than individual mental attitude towards a value-object. Instead of asserting that an actual emotion is directed towards the object, it seems to assert that the object itself *deserves* to be valued, that it *ought* to arouse approval, respect, admiration, etc., that it has value which is "valid" for all men. The notion of "validity", which is implicit in

all higher value-judgements, must either be explained
psychologically or asserted to be a mistaken notion
about something which has no actuality, if the psychological theory about Value is to be consistently maintained.

"Value" was first used as a descriptive category in the
psychological study of personality by Benecke. Under
the influence of Dilthey, its use has been definitely
established among exponents of "geisteswissenschaft-
liche" psychology of the "Struktur" school. The
peculiarity of this school of psychological thought is the
emphasis which it lays, in contradistinction from analytical psychology, on the complex as a totality. It is
only possible to understand the elements of personality
from the point of view of the whole. Eric Stern writes:
"The unity of personality must be seen in its being
directed towards values, and only from this central
point of view can personality be understood.... In what
a man sees 'value', especially in what he sees the highest
value of his life, that value, in fact, which makes life
important to him, that is what we must know if we
are to be capable of understanding his personality".[1]
Spranger, a follower of Dilthey, has used the concept of
"Value" as a basis upon which to draw up a descriptive
schema of the types of personality.[2] Among English
psychologists James Ward anticipated but did not work
out this line of approach. "It is 'the good, which every
soul pursues' that is the supreme clue to all the intricacies of psychical development." "His personality,

[1] "New Ways of Investigating the Problem of Personality", "Psyche",
iii, 358 ff.
[2] "Lebensformen."

then, will not be shewn merely in what a man is but in what he is striving to be."[1]

The essential point for our purpose here is the conception of personality as being oriented towards certain ideals of value. In the organisation, development, and unification of personality these ideals are regulative. The *direction* of sentiments and emotional dispositions is determined by them. And from them the natural and instinctive desires and passions are graded and valued.[2]

This conception carries us, within the sphere of psychology, a considerable distance beyond plain desire. In the light of an ideal, primitive conations and dispositions, even the whole assemblage of desires and emotions which analytically constitutes my actual personality, may be "valued". Nor is this valuation simply an act of intellectual comparison. For associated with the ideal is an emotion at a "higher" psychological level than desire, which I shall call "approval". Actions or desires, or empirical personality as a whole, may become the object of approval or disapproval.

Approval differs from all other emotions in that they have a relative degree of strength or impulsion while approval is associated with a *sense of obligation*. From the objective point of view of the external observer the feeling of obligation may be said to have a certain strength comparable to that of desires in so far as, when it is in conflict with desire, sometimes it and sometimes the desire determines the ensuing action. But from the point of view of immediate experience the impulsion of the feeling of obligation is different in kind from, and

[1] "Psychological Principles", chaps. xvii and xviii.
[2] See A. F. Shand, "The Foundations of Character".

incommensurable with, the impulsion of desire. Whatever be the urgency of the desire which determines
action, and however weak the feeling of obligation
which condemns the action, we still can say "I ought to
have done otherwise". The psychological fact indicated
in such "ought"-propositions is ultimate and unanalysable.

I think that the feeling of obligation is absolute in
another sense also. I often desire several things, the
attainment of which involves incompatible lines of
conduct. When this happens my actions are, as a rule,
determined by the relative strength and urgency of my
desires. I may desire one thing and feel obligation towards a line of conduct which is incompatible with the
satisfaction of my desire. When this happens my actions
may be determined either by desire or by feeling of
obligation. But I cannot feel obligation to perform two
incompatible actions and have to choose between two
"feelings of obligation". In any set of circumstances and
at any one moment I can feel obliged only to one line of
conduct. This statement needs, I think, some qualifica-
tion. When I examine the feeling of obligation in itself
alone I seem to detect that it has in its nature essentially
this absolute character. But I also seem to detect cases
where I experience a feeling of obligation to perform
incompatible actions. The explanation is to be found in
the fact that the statement that the feeling of obligation
is absolute is completely true only of the ideal or completely unified personality. It is in the nature of the
feeling to be absolute: but persons as we know them are
not completely unified; they retain conflicting and in-
completely co-ordinated elements in their ideals.

This theory of personality is consistent with either a psychological or a non-naturalistic theory about Value. If used with a psychological theory it will enable us to transcend the elementary levels of desire-valuing and explain the peculiar feeling of impulsion and obligatoriness which is exerted by valuation at the higher levels. Value is defined as the property of being held to be ideal for myself. The peculiar sense of *rightness* which I feel in admiring Gaudier's Fawn rather than the lions in Trafalgar Square, the peculiar sense of *obligation* which I feel to behave decently rather than self-interestedly, are explained with reference to the peculiar emotion which is attendant upon the conception of the Ideal.

It is not part of my present purpose to enter into the intricacies of the psychological explanation of "ideal valuation". This has been done adequately by Urban;[1] and the construction of personality has been ably described by Shand.[2] The explanation seems to me, so far forth, to be successful. But an ideal is valid only for that person whose ideal it is and for other persons so far as they share it. As Ward says: "to be personal, the ideal for which he strives must be his own; must originate in himself however impersonal its goal may be". The psychological obligation attendant upon an ideal does not transfer from one person to another except in virtue of empirical uniformity of ideals.

On the other hand, the value-judgements which we make in ethics and aesthetics do seem to have validity extending beyond the individual. When I say that Frank Dobson's "Truth" has aesthetic value I do not only mean

[1] "Valuation, its Nature and Laws."
[2] Op. cit.

that I and persons like myself approve of its admiring contemplation and disapprove of my landlady's admiration for The Soul's Awakening or the Londonderry Air. The least that the judgement implies is that there is a certain rightness in the former attitude, which is valid for all men, and that there is a wrongness or inappropriateness about the latter attitude, which is valid for all men. In ethical judgements again, when conduct is judged to be right the judgement seems not to involve reference to any particular ideal but at the least to assert an obligation for all men of given capacity in appropriate circumstances.

Psychological theories about Value have often been elaborated to unnecessary complexity with the professed intention of bringing this apparent normative validity of value-judgements in aesthetics, ethics or religion within the field of psychological explanation. But if it exists it lies logically outside the confines of psychological theory; the most that psychology could do is to explain the origin of the erroneous belief that such validity exists. In psychology each individual's own personal ideal and conscience is the ultimate source of all normative valuation for that person. The rightness which my aesthetic judgements seem to me to possess is psychologically conditioned by their conformity with my own aesthetic ideal. The intensity of my conviction of their rightness is simply the measure of their identification with my individuality. Psychology affords no ground for the assertion that they have validity for any other person except in so far as his aesthetic ideal corresponds in fact with my own, or for the assertion that my landlady's aesthetic judgements, which differ radically from mine, are wrong where mine are right. It is sometimes stated that the one ideal in aesthetics (ethics or religion) is the source of greater enjoyment or fuller experience than any other, and it is argued that it is justified on this ground. The proof of the statement has not yet been found. In any case it is irrelevant in this place, because it depends upon a particular value-judgement (enjoyment or fullness of experience is more valuable than any other thing) and does not affect the theory about the nature of Value itself. A psychologist may deny the reality of the apparent unconditioned rightness of the value-judgements of which we are speaking, and may offer a psychological explanation of the prevalence of the illusion; but he cannot both admit that rightness and reduce it to terms of individual psychology. Either the psychological definition of Value is inadequate, or the "rightness" of value-judgements in aesthetics, ethics and religion is limited by its reference to particular individuals or groups of individuals with similar ideals.

Some writers accept this view and admit that Value because psychologically conditioned is ultimately individualistic. This is not only an admission that the ultimate standard we have for the comparison of valuations is the personal ideal of each individual (that may be true upon any theory about Value), but it is an admission that the statement that my valuations are "better" or "more right" than another person's is meaningless or tautologous. It is tautologous if it means that they are better for me; it is meaningless unless it means this. If I say that my own aesthetic taste is "better" than my landlady's, all I mean is that if she were more like me she would appreciate more as I do. If I say that my notions of good and bad conduct are "better" or "more right" than those of an habitual criminal, all I mean is that if he were more like me he would judge more as I do. The distinction between "good Taste" and personal taste, the distinction of higher and lower levels of morality, in fact all evaluation of character is the vulgar assertiveness either of personal prejudice or of collective snobbery.

That view has the great merit that it encourages tolerance and strikes at the roots of fanaticism and all self-importance. And it leaves the valuations and ideals of all individuals as they are. Were it universally believed, the missionary would be on the rolls of the unemployed and propaganda must sail under the flag of self-interest. Some people would, indeed, from our present accepted standpoint degenerate in character. For just as the consciousness that our beliefs and valuations are shared by many other people gives them, however unreasonably, additional authority for us; so the valuations of many people seem to be very closely bound up with the belief that they are a representation, albeit imperfect at some points, of objectively valid and psychologically un-conditioned values and obligations. Were that belief destroyed, such people would find it difficult even to retain their existing ideals. But this would not matter, because there is no standard of value objective to and independent of the actual ideals of individuals. So as the ideals altered valuableness would alter.

Other philosophers have endeavoured to find a solution less objectionable to common sense and their own beliefs, while remaining loyal to the psychological definition of Value, by a theory of the social origin of valuation. This theory shall now be examined.

CHAPTER VIII

SUBJECTIVE THEORIES (b) SOCIAL

THE explanation of Value by means of social psychology has been stated with much minuteness and elaboration by Professor Urban and with praiseworthy clarity and terseness by Dr Tennant.[1] Since our purpose is to examine its logical foundations rather than its most intricate ramifications, we shall follow Dr Tennant's statement.

Dr Tennant is a pupil and admirer of James Ward, and is firmly attached to the *genetic* psychology which Ward popularised in England and Baldwin in America. Genetic psychology endeavours to explain the psychological processes of the normal socialised person of to-day by tracing the development of self-consciousness, intelligence and affective-conational dispositions from the primitive unsocialised and unself-conscious individual, whose field of awareness is limited by his own private world of sensations. Now Psychology is the most difficult of all sciences in which to apply the idea of development, for there are no tangible records of the past with which to check theorisation. The primitive individual, who reacts only by simple desire and aversion to his immediate sensations and who has not the conception of an objective world of things external to himself, is a psychological fiction. It may be a correct representation of the facts; such an individual may have

[1] Urban, "Valuation, its Nature and Laws". F. R. Tennant, "Philosophical Theology", i, chap. vii.

existed. But certain it is, that he no longer exists to check the suppositions of the psychologist. Nor can the stages of evolution which are postulated to have intervened between this primitive individual and the socialised individual of to-day be tested against a background of fact. One can but admire the success which was achieved by this psychology when one considers that the task which it set itself was to explain something which is present before us to be observed and examined, by a theory of development which must always remain imaginary and unverifiable. Even if the primitive individual of the genetic psychologist were to exist he could not communicate to us his psychological processes. Genetic psychology has waged a gallant war against the heritage in modern psychology of the individualism of Herbart and Hume; but now that the victory is assured, and there is no longer a serious danger of the importance of the social aspect of individual psychology being neglected, much of its usefulness has vanished. In any consideration the utility of a theory of psychological development must always be confined to the light which it can throw upon the psychology of the developed person of to-day. It should not be ascribed an archaeological or historical importance akin to that of evolutionary theories in biology, which can be checked by fossilised remains, etc., and are built up upon a basis, however slender, of observed facts.

We should, then, need to discount anything in Dr Tennant's theory which was directly dependent upon an unprovable conception of psychological development. But in fact his use of genetic psychology colours his statement of his theory about value rather than the

theory itself. And indeed genetic psychology affords a
not inconvenient mode of exposition for one who defines
value as the object of desire, admits higher and lower
grades of value, but is unwilling to introduce any extra-
psychological element into the definition of value.

Dr Tennant first defines value as the property of being
an object of desire. At the lowest level of the merely per-
cipient and conative being, "valuable" means "desired".
From this, by the principles of genetic psychology, he
would explain the notion of "the categorical imperative
'I ought'; in which obligation and law are inward and
apparently unconditional; in which goodness is no
longer desiredness, by some one or many, of what is
good for something, but is conceived as an intrinsic
quality of desiredness or of oughtness-to-be, independent
of the conation, and even the cognition, of all persons".

Two stages of advance are distinguished in the sphere
of individual psychology. The first is the advance from
immediate response of desire or aversion, to prudential
judgements. "The self is, in fact, the condition and the
standard of all primitive evaluation, and self-interest
emerges with the rudimentary knowledge of self.
Thenceforward, blind preference between pleasures—i.e.
pleasure-able objects—determined simply by intensity of
feeling, can give place to choice that is intellectually
grounded. Self-interest prompts deliberation; and some
scale of values, according to psychological rank, can be
established by individual experience, though of course
but for it alone. When one has learned that what is good
to eat is not always wholesome, intelligence alone makes
possible a preference of the abiding pleasure of health
to the fleeting, if intenser, enjoyment of a flavour." The

second stage is, as it seems to me, more important; with it emerges the rudimentary beginning of Conscience. As self-consciousness grows, the actions, dispositions and character of the individual himself can become objects of his intellectual contemplation and awake in him feeling and conation. He can discriminate an *Ideal* Self (himself as he would be) from his actual Self (himself as he is). This is somewhat obscurely expressed by Dr Tennant, as follows: "When, however, the inner and ideal 'self' has been discriminated from the bodily and appetitive 'self', interests can also be organised in respect of their inwardness. Psychologically, a pleasure of 'higher' value to an individual, is one to which value is assigned only at a psychologically higher level of self-hood or self-knowledge. We always and inevitably prefer a more pleasurable, to a less pleasurable experience; but as the self grows, the pleasures to be weighed do not remain the same *for it*". Now this discrimination of "values for the self" at different "levels" seems to me essentially to involve the taking up of an attitude of approval or disapproval towards the self or certain aspects of the self. And in self-approval and disapproval I am inclined to place the origin of *moral* approbation. Although this still remains within the psychological sphere of satisfaction or desire, there is here surely the emergence of a new *type* of feeling, a feeling which *as experienced* (*erlebt*) and in its emotional tone, is unique, and different from any feeling of desire or conation that is experienced below this level of self-hood. In fact, it is here that Conscience emerges. It is to be wished that Dr Tennant had made more of this emergence.

We are still within the region of *individual* valuation

(value for the individual); only the value-object has developed from being merely an object of bodily perception to being a state of the self and ideal for the self. And, I suggest, a new type of feeling (self-approbation and disapprobation) constitutive of value has emerged in relation to this "higher" type of value-object. We now proceed along a different line of development towards social value and obligation. Through the community of human interests and desires the individual can arrive at judgements of the form "good for society". "Though, perhaps, no two individuals are constituted psychologically alike, none are altogether different. None are isolated; in virtue of certain extra-regarding interests and desires, none are originally pure egoists; none unfamiliar with social restraint. Hence the possibility of some community of desire, and of co-operation towards a common end, is ensured." These facts "indicate the possibility of advance—from the good, in the sense of what is desired by a self for itself, to the good as what is desired by an organic whole, composed of a plurality of more or less co-operant and consentient selves". Among the objects of such social value-judgements ("valuable for society") may be the self and its actions (i.e. I may say "I am a socially valuable or socially useless person"). Such social judgements, however, are not yet within the sphere of *obligation*; they are, or may be, intellectual only; they have no motive force ensuring "the spontaneous subordination of private interest to common weal". I have still to judge that I *ought* to be a socially valuable person when my private interests conflict with the public weal. This motive force Dr Tennant finds in altruism. "The human individual does

4-2

not enter into social life a pure egoist, who has somehow
to acquire self-denial and approval of it. When conscience
is thrust upon him he already knowns sympathy. There
are propensities ingrained in human nature which
prompt to altruism. ... There remains, then, no mystery
about the emergence of conscience such as acknowledges indebtedness or feels inward obligation, as well as
yields external compliance to social duty."

In order to facilitate reference to a rather complicated
exposition I will re-state the theory in tabular form.

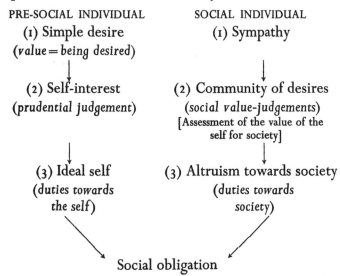

PRE-SOCIAL INDIVIDUAL   SOCIAL INDIVIDUAL
(1) Simple desire   (1) Sympathy
(value = being desired)

(2) Self-interest   (2) Community of desires
(prudential judgement)   (social value-judgements)
                               [Assessment of the value of the
                               self for society]

(3) Ideal self   (3) Altruism towards society
(duties towards   (duties towards
the self)   society)

Social obligation

One step remains to be taken to reach the "absolute
obligation" of pure ethics. "When 'I owe' is no longer
acknowledged to the Actual self or to contemporary
society, but to an idealisation of the self, to an idealised
society, or to God; and when an ideal law is constructed
out of current *mores*, in a way similar to that in which
the triangle in geometry is distilled—by idealising and

abstracting—out of the visible surface: the sense of obligation necessarily becomes inward and unconditioned. 'I owe' is transmuted, in virtue of its new intellectual or existential presupposition, into 'I ought'. Further abstractive intellection can eliminate both the lawgiver and the I, and so arrive at the bare concept of 'oughtness-to-be': which is determinative of ethics proper, according to one view."

It is claimed that this theory accounts for all value-judgements, including ethical judgements; and it does so without postulating a notion of Value which is logically antecedent to any psychical attitude towards the object valued. We must examine it in order to test the claim that it accounts for all value-judgements.

Let us first investigate more closely the assertion that all values are psychologically grounded or conditioned. It may mean either or both of two things. (1) It may mean to affirm that only actual or ideal states of human beings, and states of affairs in which these are organically contained as constituents, may be truly asserted to be valuable; that value-objects always either are or contain psychological states. This affirmation is not a definition of Value and carries no prima facie implication as to the meaning of the value-judgement. To it the Realist or the Idealist might subscribe without hesitation. Professor Sorley, indeed, does expressly subscribe to it. He holds, for instance, that not Truth but the concrete apprehension of true propositions as true, not Beauty but the concrete appreciation of beautiful objects, have value. When he has proved this, the exponent of a psychological theory about the nature of Value has proved nothing of advantage to his theory. (2) It may mean to affirm that valuableness is relation to mental attitude; that the proposition which asserts that "X has value" *means* the assertion "X stands in a certain relation to human interests and ideals"; that it means this and nothing more; that it does *not* mean the assertion "X *ought* to stand in a certain relation to human interests and ideals"; in fine, that the notion of "ought" logically prior to human interests and ideals is an empty notion with no meaning at all. This, and not the former, proposition must be proved by those who hold a psychological theory about Value.

It is necessary to exercise considerable caution in order not to confuse these two affirmations. Both are of interest, but we are concerned only with the latter. For we are concerned to investigate the nature of the quality Value and not to plot a chart of the incidence of value in the geography of existence. We must also remember that discussions of the "geography" of value are logically subsequent to, and have no direct bearing upon, theory about the nature of Value. We have then to examine the psychological theory about Value as a theory about the nature of Value, and statements that all objects which possess value are, or contain, psychological states, are not directly relevant.

In the first place, the theory does succeed in grounding psychologically the difference between judgements of the form "I desire" and judgements of the form "I ought". The "feeling of obligation" which is directed towards a personal ideal, and which is genetically attendant upon psychological discrimination of the actual self from the ideal self, has a different emotional tone from the feeling of pure desire, arouses conation and aspiration, and gives rise to the judgement "I ought". Thus the proposition "I ought to do X" *means* "I have a feeling of obligation towards X" or "X is the object of a feeling of obligation experienced by me". Secondly, in virtue of "social altruism", social objects or ideals, such for example as Justice or The Common Welfare of Humanity, may become the objects towards which my feeling of obligation is directed. If the "ideal self" which I aspire to become is a self which has the maximum of social utility, I shall feel obliged, and judge that I ought, on all occasions to subordinate my private interests to the good of society. If necessary, I shall be prepared to sacrifice my life for the furtherance of the good of humanity. Thus all judgements of the form "I ought" are, I think, successfully accounted for. Are these all that we need to account for?

There are in common use judgements which have the apparent form "all men ought". Whenever we ethically criticise or approve of another man we make implicit reference to such a judgement. Whether I say "that is the best man I know", or "that man behaved unethically on such and such an occasion", or "that man's character is ethically bad", I am using a standard which is antecedently valid for all men. That this is so will be shown by the consideration that judgements of the form "All men ought to do this" do not simply mean "all men do in fact experience a feeling of obligation to do this". If that were all that they meant ethical criticism and comparison of ethical standards would be impossible. Moreover, they would be most obviously untrue: there is not actual uniformity as to the objects towards which the feelings of obligation experienced by individuals are directed. These judgements must mean one of three things: (1) all men do actually experience a feeling of obligation towards such and such a thing; (2) it is conducive to the welfare of society that all men should experience a feeling of obligation to do such and such a thing; (3) there is an absolute and psychologically unconditioned obligation for all men to do such and such a thing. We have seen that they do not mean the first of these alternatives; the third is expressly denied as inconsistent with the psychological definition of Value. Do they mean the second?

In virtue of the community of interests and aspirations of a group of co-operant and consentient beings it is possible intellectually to conceive objects and ideals of the group as a group—*social* objects and ideals. These have been called "social values". Indeed the intellectual apprehension of "social values" is a presupposition of altruism at the social level, for I cannot experience a feeling of obligation, in virtue of my ideal for myself, to promote social values until I have reached intellectually the notion of social values. The conception of "social value" requires, then, to be investigated. It is a peculiarity of the structure of the psychological value-judgement ("X has value *for* Y") that it always includes a specific reference; and the reference may not be to the person who makes the judgement. A certain man "A" may form a judgement about the value of an object X for *another man* Y. Such a judgement obviously does *not* mean that A experiences any emotional attitude of valuing towards X; it means that Y, in the opinion of A, experiences such an attitude—that and nothing more. Now judgements about *social* value are really compendious judgements summarising a vast number of particular judgements of the form "A judges X has (actual, dispositional, or potential) value for Y". For "society" is not an independent existent and has no being apart from the concrete individuals (past, present, and perhaps future) of which it is composed. As, then, A's judgement "X has value for Y" implies nothing about A's emotional attitudes towards X and does not imply that X has value for A, so A's judgement "X is socially valuable" does not imply that X has value for A. After I have judged "X is socially valuable" X *may*, in virtue of my social altruism, become an object of desire for me or even an object of my feeling of obligation. But it equally well may not. Yet so long as we adhere to a psychological definition of Value, the proposition "I ought to do what is socially valuable" *can only mean* "I experience a feeling of obligation to do what is socially valuable". I suspect that most exponents of the psychological theory of Value have unconsciously confused the propositions "X is socially valuable" and "every individual member of a society ought to promote X". But *except in virtue of a sense of obligation experienced by each particular individual* it is impossible to proceed from the former proposition to the latter. Psychical beings are essentially and ultimately discrete; if "ought" is defined in relation to psychical states, it is impossible to ascribe obligation on the part of one person on the grounds of psychical states occurring in other persons.

We must, then, examine the implications of the interpretation that judgements of the form "all men ought to do such and such a thing" mean simply "it would be socially valuable if all men experienced feelings of obligation to do such and such a thing". This position is logically tenable and, if I am right, the only position which can be maintained consistently with a psychological theory about the nature of Value. It is not conformable to popular and commonsense beliefs; but popular and commonsense beliefs may be wrong. First it follows from it that the proposition "all men ought to experience a sense of obligation to do what is socially valuable" is nugatory: it means only "it would be socially valuable if all men experienced a sense of obligation to do what is socially valuable". Hence the only criterion for comparison between the moral sense of individuals, and the only basis for the discussion of moral duties, is their conduciveness to the realisation of common and shared aspirations and interests. That is, a utility basis. It is a fact of history that individuals exist from time to time with a fairly clear apprehension of the socially valuable but with little impulse, or none at all, to produce it. The a-moral intellectual and the "social sadist" are, fortunately, uncommon. But they are only the extremes which illustrate the principle. Within the confines of the normal there are various degrees of subordination of personal to social ends. Discussing ultimate moral ends, Dr Tennant finds an irreducible duality between the duty of self-realisation and duty to society. This is probably the practical discovery of all normal men. But on the one side stands the a-moral intellectual and on the other the sentimental humanitarian, who recognises only duty to society. These and all other differences between individual consciences can be judged only by *social utility* unless we are prepared to abandon a psychological theory of Value.

These corollaries of the theory have not been recognised by all its exponents. In fact they have not been realised except by superficial writers who have started with the conviction of the essential relativity or essential insignificance of ethical judgements. They have been obscured by the interaction of two confusions: (1) the confusion between some property of the class of objects which may be characterised by value and the nature of Value itself (all value-objects are psychologically grounded: therefore Value is psychologically conditioned); (2) the confusion between social value and individual obligation (X is socially valuable; therefore every individual ought to promote the existence of X).

A further consequence arises out of the above, relative to the discrimination of "higher" and "lower" values. Either the gradation of "higher–lower" is based upon the psychological complexity of the psychical state which is constitutive of the value in question, and so has no ethical import; or it is relative to this or that individual and has no universal application. For any discrimination of "higher–lower" in respect of *valuableness* must be relative to the valuational attitudes of this or that individual or group of individuals. A relation originating *within* a system cannot be applied from a point *outside* the system as a principle of discrimination among the members of the system. If Value is a relation subsisting between certain existents N_1, N_2, ... and particular individuals A, B, C, ... it cannot *also* be a principle by which N_1, N_2, may be graded according to rank, without reference to A, B, C.... In fact, many writers have surreptitiously introduced a *non*-psychological concept of Value with their gradation "higher–lower". In the preliminary account of the scope of his work Mr Perry writes: "It would be the task of such a theory of value first to bring to light the underlying principle common to these sciences [scil. the sciences of the special fields of value], and then to employ this principle for the purpose of arbitrating between them". Mr Perry has forgotten that a common principle cannot be a principle of discrimination. Dr Tennant warns us that he is describing genetic evolution. But does he not incline to presume that the genesis of a "higher" psychological level (i.e. psychologically more complex, or psychologically later, and psychologically new) is the mark of a "higher" level of value? Be that as it may, it is certain that from a psychological theory of value levels of valuableness cannot be discriminated except for this or that individual or group. I may estimate my own aspirations and ethical attitudes, and those of people like myself, as more valuable for me than the aspirations and the ethical attitudes of the primitive savage or the moron with a bent for criminality. I can judge them to be more conducive to the welfare of a particular type of society. But I cannot judge them to be better or more valuable except for myself and people like myself. I cannot say that I am right and the savage is wrong when he prefers his own morals to mine. For we are asserting different things and not the same thing, he a comparison between the relations in which his morals and mine stand to his moral conscience and I a comparison between the relations in which they stand to mine. Thus either "ethical comparison", "gradation of values", "progress", etc. must be reduced to a non-ethical principle such as complexity or they must be referred to a particular point of view and there will be no unifying principle superordinate to the manifold points of view of discrete individuals or groups.

I hold it to be certain that neither the considerations which I have advanced, nor any considerations that could be advanced, suffice to disprove the psychological theory about Value. They do not even tend to disprove it. But they show that it can be consistently maintained only at the expense of complete ethical relativity. So long as we adhere to the psychological theory about the nature of Value, we can assert value or obligation only for this person or that person and only on the basis of the mental processes of the person for whom they are asserted. Further, we can estimate or evaluate the characters of the persons for whom we assert these values and obligations to exist only from the point of view of this, that or the other person. There can be no ultimate principle by which we could harmonise and evaluate the valuations of scattered individuals. For such a principle must necessarily be logically antecedent to psychical processes. For if it were not logically antecedent to psychical processes it would be dependent upon the psychical processes of this or that individual, and we should once more be brought back to the individual point of view.

But this ultimate relativity may be consistently affirmed. True, it does not seem to be consistent with the unconscious presuppositions of mankind. We do seem to make judgements about an obligation antecedent to psychical attitudes, judgements involving the proposition "All men ought...". Yet these judgements may always be, what they indubitably often are, emblems of that vulgarity in socialised and herded man, which causes him to impose those ideals and obligations which he recognises as valid for himself upon others also as valid and obligatory for them. This noxious tendency exists and will continue to exist, particularly among the professed upholders of a generation-old social moral. But even here discrimination may be introduced. The Englishman recognises a peculiarly national obligation to "fair play" and endeavours with a sense of his own ethical superiority to impose that obligation upon persons of other nationality whose ideals of conduct differ in any respect from his conception of "fair play". The English artist has no serious temptations to extend the obligation to develop one's own artistic talents to all men, or even to all Englishmen. Yet the English artist may, in a cool moment, consider his obligation to develop his own artistic talents to the full to be superior to his obligation to "fair play".

But such considerations as these may be bandied on this side and on that interminably. It is impossible by empirical investigation to prove or disprove ethical relativity. I believe also that ethical relativity cannot be proved or disproved by any logical argument. It could, perhaps, be proved or disproved from the assumption of a general metaphysic of Reality: but I know no general metaphysic of Reality, from the assumption of which it could be proved or disproved, and which does not itself implicitly assume either ethical relativity or its converse. Here leaving this matter I shall proceed with an investigation of other theories about Value; in the conviction, however, both that no one except a philosopher would maintain a theory of unrestricted ethical relativity while clearly understanding its import, and also that few of the philosophers who have held a psychological theory about Value would continue to hold that theory were they to realise that it logically involved them in ultimate ethical relativity.

CHAPTER IX

REALISM

R EALISM about Value I take to be the theory that the notion of intrinsic value, as it has been carefully defined by Professor G. E. Moore in his essay on "The Conception of Intrinsic Value", is a meaningful notion and that intrinsic values do exist.

Intrinsic valuableness is a quality which depends solely upon the intrinsic nature of the object which it characterises. "To say that a kind of value is 'intrinsic' means merely that the question whether a thing possesses it, and in what degree it possesses it, depends solely on the intrinsic nature of the thing in question." From which it follows that "A kind of value is 'intrinsic' if and only if, when anything possesses it, that same thing or anything exactly like it would *necessarily* or *must* always under all circumstances, possess it in exactly the same degree".[1] The "necessity" in question is said to be neither causal necessity (universality in *fact*) nor logical implication. It is the kind of necessity which we assert to hold, when we say that "if a given patch of colour be yellow, then any patch which were exactly like the first would be yellow too".

But although intrinsic valuableness is dependent *solely* upon the intrinsic nature of the object which possesses it, it is not itself a natural or an intrinsic quality. It does not, like intrinsic properties, *constitute* or *describe* the intrinsic nature of what possesses it. "If you could enumerate

[1] "Philosophical Studies", pp. 260, 265.

all the intrinsic properties a given thing possessed, you would have a *complete* description of it, and would not need to mention any predicates of value it possessed; whereas no description of a given thing could be *complete* which omitted any intrinsic property."[1] In this way realism is distinguished from those forms of naturalism which hold valuableness to be an intrinsic quality.

I do not think that any fault can be found with Professor Moore's statement unless it is with the parallel he draws to the kind of *necessity* he postulates in his statement. The necessity which we assert to hold when we say that "if a given patch of colour be yellow, then any patch which were exactly like the first would be yellow" seems to be purely verbal. The meaning of the words "exactly alike" is "not differing in any respect" and the exclusion of difference in general involves the inclusion of all particular differences. As difference in respect of colour is a difference, we should not apply the words "exactly alike" to two patches of colour one of which was yellow and the other not yellow. But when Professor Moore uses "exactly alike" in his description of the meaning of intrinsic Value, he uses it in the sense "exactly alike in respect of intrinsic qualities" and not in the sense "exactly alike in respect of intrinsic qualities *and of degree of value*". Thus in the second passage quoted he is stating *more* than the verbal necessity "if X is Y (and Y by definition excludes Z), X is without Z". Were the parallel exact we should be entitled to assert only that if two things are not exactly alike in respect of value then at least in respect of value they are not exactly alike. If the parallel is *not* exact we have no clue to the sort of

[1] "Philosophical Studies", p. 274.

"necessity" Prof. Moore posits. The facts he affirms seem to be obviously true. But his conception of Value precludes an explanation of why they are true.

Moore holds, then, that Value is a "simple, indefinable, unanalysable object of thought". We have immediate non-sensuous apprehension of its concrete nature. And we have immediate intuitive knowledge of its presence, and the degree and sense (positive or negative) in which it is present, to particular things. I have been able to find two arguments only by which he endeavours to recommend this position.[1] One of them is certain but irrelevant; the other is relevant but not certain.

He first points out at some length that "pleasure", "the object of desire" etc. are not definitions of the abstract quality "good", but names of certain classes of concrete facts which have been alleged from time to time to possess that quality. "The good", or that which is good, is not identical with the goodness by which it is characterised. Valuableness and value-object are not the same thing. An attribute is not identical with the class of objects of which it can be predicated. The mistake of identifying a class-quality with the class of things to which it belongs was a commonplace with Plato, and should not now constitute a serious menace in philosophy.

Whether any philosopher has seriously meant to identify "goodness" with the class of "good things" I do not know: there has no doubt been much verbal ambiguity among certain ethical writers. But the clearing up of this elementary confusion has no bearing at all upon naturalistic theories which define valuableness as

[1] "Principia Ethica", chap. i.

"the property of being an object of my interest", etc. Still less has it any tendency to prove that the notion of Value is indefinable. Moore confuses the fallacy of identifying an attribute with the class of things of which it is predicable, and the "naturalistic" fallacy (definition of valuableness in terms of psychological or empirical fact)—which really is not a fallacy at all. It may quite consistently be maintained that when we say "value" or "good" we do mean simply the existence or possibility of a peculiar kind of relation between mind and object. Moore's later criticism of psychological ethical theories consists in the main in showing that their exponents have as a matter of fact used "good" in a normative and non-natural sense and that this use is inconsistent with a naturalistic definition of goodness. It is probably true that no ethical theory has yet been stated with perfect consistency on naturalistic lines. If this is so it would render plausible the supposition that those who hold naturalistic theories of Value do shut their eyes to an aspect of reality which, if admitted to exist, is enormously important. But even were it proved that all ethical theories have made use of an indefinable notion of "oughtness", and assumed that all ethical theories must in the future make use of this notion, the indefinability of Value would not thereby be proved. For valuableness could, with perfect consistency and considerable plausibility, be defined in reference to a normative non-natural relation, viz. valuableness means "oughtness or worthiness to be desired" (Sorley), "oughtness to be loved" (Brentano).

The argument which is pertinent to the point contested (that "good" is indefinable) occurs on pp. 15 f. It is given incidentally and is not, I believe, conclusive.

5-2

I will state the argument in general terms: In whatever way Value is defined, it will always be possible to find at least one state of affairs which is not characterised by the property or properties alleged to constitute valuableness, but which may significantly be made the subject of a synthetic value-proposition (*i.e.* which is valuable or disvaluable). Therefore the class of things of which valuableness can be significantly predicated (i.e. the class of value-objects) is not identical with the class of things which is characterised by any other property or properties whatsoever. Therefore valuableness cannot be analytically defined. In illustration is taken the definition of goodness as "the property of being a thing which I desire to desire". Then I can significantly ask, "Is my desire to desire good?" But I cannot significantly ask, "Do I desire to desire to desire to desire?" because I do not have before my mind such a complicated state of affairs as my "desire to desire to desire to desire". Therefore the class of things which I hold to be positively or negatively valuable is not identical with the class of things which I desire to desire or not to desire.

I think this argument may be valid against the definition of Value as the property of being a thing which I desire to desire. But I do not know that anyone has seriously maintained this definition. We have, however, only to find *one* definition of Value which is not open to this objection, and the argument is disproved. For it is an argument depending upon negation. The feeling of approval is admitted to be a psychical state and may be constitutive of Value. If it were so then the proposition "X is valuable" would mean "A feels approval for X". Now I may, from the platform of age and experience

look back upon the moral attitudes of my earlier years
and experience a feeling of approval for my youthful
approval for X. That means that my youthful approval for
X has value for me now. Can we go a stage further back
and feel approval for our approval for our approval for X?
I leave the question to the ingenuity of practised introspec-
tionists of ripe years. But I would assert that we can feel
approval for *another man's* approval for his or my approval
for X. So the argument leads us back into the complexities
of introspection; and he would be a rash man who would
affirm that I must cease to *approve* of approval... for X
before I can cease to say "my approval... for X has
value" or "is good". Before, then, he is entitled to assert
that "whatever definition be offered, it may always be
asked, with significance, of the complex so defined,
whether it is itself good", Prof. Moore must be able to
refute *this* definition ("goodness" means to be a thing of
which I approve) and *any* other definition that is advanced.
That he refutes the peculiar definition which he himself
has chosen has not the faintest tendency to prove his
general negation.

As a matter of fact Moore himself discredits his
argument when he envisages the possibility that pleasure
may be a universal concomitant of value. (Surely he
should have said "*pleasantness* is a universal concomitant
of apprehended value"?) For if everything that is
valuable is also pleasant (pleasure-causing) to the person
who apprehends its value it will not be possible to find
anything which has value but which is not the object of
a pleasurable state. Hence the argument would not be
valid against the definition of Value as "the property of
being the object of a pleasurable mental state". Hence

a *negative* criterion to distinguish between valuableness and conduciveness to pleasure, is useless: they can only be discriminated by an intuitive or immediate acquaintance with the positive nature of valuableness. Such a positive turn is given to the argument on p. 16, where the predicate "good" is said to be known by inspection to be "positively different" from the predicate "being an object which I desire to desire" or from any other predicate at all. Here then is the crux of the matter. The argument is ultimately dependent upon an immediate acquaintance with the positive nature of valuableness; it rests upon an appeal to inspection. Intuition of Value is not merely knowledge *about* value (i.e. its distribution among existing things), but must also be immediate acquaintance with the positive or concrete nature of the quality "valuableness".

Now the majority of philosophers who have given the matter their best attention have professed themselves to be unable to become acquainted with any such positive content, and have consequently rejected the notion of a pure indefinable value-quality.[1] The point is unarguable. In the perception of colours there is a standard of normality, deviation from which can usually be traced to physical abnormality. But in the apprehension of values there is far less unanimity and the organ of perception is intellectual not sensual. In a disagreement about primary data, which are, moreover, immediately apprehended, there may be a high degree of individual certitude but there can be no logical certainty. But when the appeal is to immediate inspection and the bulk of philosophical opinion is certainly unfavourable, dog-

[1] Cf. Tennant, op. cit. p. 158.

matism is singularly out of place. Adherents of both theories have, in general, tended to assess their theory by their personal and private certitude and not by its logical certainty. And here, in essence, must this matter rest.

As I considered the unsatisfactoriness of this conclusion, it occurred to me that perhaps a compromise might be reached by examining the opinions about the class of *objects characterised by Value.* Did the Realists agree in seposing a class of objects as value-objects, and did this class correspond to no class of objects which could be clearly demarcated upon any psychological basis, it would be more reasonable to suppose that they were possessed of a veridical faculty of value-intuition not possessed by the majority of philosophers, than it would be reasonable to suppose this were they not agreed upon any such class.

The question of the distribution of value presents no theoretical complications for a psychological theory about Value. Every psychosis or Seelenaugenblick (Rehmke) contains affective and volitional constituents. Therefore any state of affairs that can become the object of a psychosis (*Gegenstand*) is potentially a value-object. And if no two persons are ever exactly alike in their psychical constitution, the distribution of value will not be exactly the same for any two persons. For realistic theories the distribution of value is apprehended intuitively and therefore cannot be argued about. The only question that arises is the measure of agreement which in fact exists among the judgements of philosophers who maintain a realistic theory. The psychological theory only allows error in so far as there is error about the mental states of the person for whom a thing is valuable. But it is a corollary of the realistic theory that whenever disagreement about the valuableness of an object exists, at least one of the conflicting judgements is erroneous. Professor Moore has defended the plausibility, and put forward the hope, that there may be found a uniform concomitant of valuableness. But if such a concomitant were found it would be of little theoretical use, because before we could know it to be universal we should need to know by direct inspection that it existed and value existed in every object in which either of them do in fact exist. We must therefore compare the actual judgements of Realists.

The main issue between them is whether only mental states and organic wholes which contain mental constituents, are value-objects; or whether some purely physical states of affairs may have value. Professor Sorley (who writes as a realist as often as he writes as an idealist) thinks that only persons and their states or qualities can have intrinsic value. He confesses a doubt, however, in respect of beautiful objects. Dr Broad thinks it "highly probable" that "no state of affairs can be good or bad unless it is or contains as a constituent some conscious mental state".[1] Professor Laird holds that "it would seem at least possible" that there might be moral values "in the absence of conscious experience", and that "the beauties of Nature might exist (and be good because beautiful) apart from a hearing ear or a beholding eye".[2] Professor Moore is certain (a) that

[1] "Mind and Its Place in Nature", p. 488.
[2] "A Study in Moral Theory", p. 100.

material states of affairs do sometimes possess a certain degree of intrinsic value; (b) that organic wholes which contain mental constituents possess a much greater degree of intrinsic value than purely material states of affairs; and (c) that the admiring contemplation of beautiful objects and the enjoyment of friendship possess a much higher degree of intrinsic value than is possessed by anything else at all. Now when he says that material states of affairs do sometimes possess a certain degree of intrinsic value, Professor Moore is, I think, envisaging beautiful objects, for they are the only example he suggests of material states possessing intrinsic value. Later in the Principia, however, he defines the beautiful as that of which the admiring contemplation is good. In other words, Beauty is the property of being an object of a specific mental attitude (admiring contemplation) which is good. Non-beautiful objects would be objects which either do not excite admiring contemplation or, if they do excite admiring contemplation, the mental state of a person admiringly contemplating them is disvaluable. I do not find this definition of Beauty satisfactory, because I think there must be some intrinsic property common to all objects which we call beautiful, and absent from all objects which we call non-beautiful, in virtue of which the admiring contemplation of the former is good and the admiring contemplation of the latter is not good. But this is by the way. If we take Moore's definition, it is not impossible that all objects which are beautiful (i.e. capable of standing in a certain relation to minds) should also be valuable intrinsically and apart from that relation to minds; but it is difficult to see why they should be thought to be so rather than the objects of any other valuable mental attitude, than the objects, for instance, of a good (and rightly directed) emotion or desire. One suspects that the author retains an unanalysed emotional attitude towards the beautiful, which goes beyond his definition. We may, then, assert a qualified agreement amongst realists that only mental states, or states of affairs which contain mental constituents, have intrinsic value. (The more agreement there were the more would the realists' position be helped.)

It is clear that this class of objects is not identical with but narrower than the class of objects which may become the objects of simple psychical processes like desire. And, so far as this argument carries weight, it would therefore seem probable that the realists are apprehending something actual and something which is not the property of "being desired". But the class of objects demarcated does appear to be identical with the class of objects towards which the "emergent" psychical process which I above termed approval may be directed. Hence it is impossible in this way to prove a probability that the realists are acquainted with an actual quality other than the property of "being an object of approval".

Although we recognise that empirical considerations cannot give logical certainty, when logical disputation has failed it is worth while to derive any guidance from empirical facts that they may give. Let us therefore turn from intuitions of a *class* of value-objects to the particular intuitions of the valuableness of existing things. Ultimate diversity of value-judgements (so long as each is judging of the valuableness of things for himself) is what the exponent of a psychological theory about Value ought to expect.

But the incompatibility which is admitted to exist among actual intuitions of intrinsic value seems to me to constitute a serious difficulty for the realist theory. It is of course true that the diversity and heterogeneity of moral beliefs which have been sincerely accredited in the past and which are held with conviction to-day, is not a fair picture of the extent of disagreement which exists and has existed between *intrinsic* value-judgements. The majority of value-judgements by which men direct their lives are instrumental, or they are accepted principles which have been acquired in nursery and school and are applied uncritically by rule of thumb. Genuine judgements about intrinsic value, asserted on the ground of personal inspection, would probably display considerably more congruity.

If a certain state of affairs is intuited as valuable by A, disvaluable by B, and non-valuable by C, of A, B and C two must be mistaken. For the same thing cannot at the same time possess and not possess the same intrinsic quality, or possess opposed intrinsic qualities. Therefore our intuitions about the distribution of value in the actual world must be fallible and in certain cases erroneous. For such disagreement does exist. This is not denied. Mr Russell's insistent endeavour to show that the amount of disagreement about intrinsic value-judgements is small, or very much less than would appear from a superficial view of the matter, combined with his admission that there is no reason to suppose our intrinsic value-judgements do not sometimes conflict, seems to presuppose that where there is a great deal of agreement, or a great deal more agreement than disagreement, intuition is probably right. For there would be little point in showing that there was a great deal of unrecognised agreement about false and incorrect judgements. But I can see no reason for this assumption except on one of two conditions. Either there must be an assignable cause for the errors of intuition of value when it errs; or there must be some reason which makes it likely that our faculty to have intuitive knowledge of the distribution of intrinsic value *usually* leads us to correct conclusions.

1. When a large number of percipients are simultaneously observing the same objective situation, and a large majority of them obtain similar percepts, while a few obtain dissimilar and incompatible percepts, it is assumed that the majority are right. But the assumption does not rest upon an *a priori* probability that the majority must be right. It is justified by the verifiable supposition that there is an assignable cause for the incompatible percepts of the few (*e.g.* malformation of the sensory organs, etc.). Much of our perceptual experience may also be *verified* by its ability to arouse expectation which is not subsequently disappointed. That test is unavailable for intuition of value. Nor can the former test be applied. Emotion or passion might prevent individuals from exercising their faculty of value-intuition in particular cases, or this faculty might in some individuals be undeveloped; but if an individual *is* intuiting value, passion or impulse cannot conceivably account for erroneous functioning of this faculty. The errors of the few cannot be traced to abnormality in any respect other than that they are unusual in their value-intuitions. Hence if passion is given as the psychological cause for errors in intuitions about value, it must be

claimed that so long as people are actually intuiting (and are not uttering passional judgements under the mistaken supposition that they are intuiting) there will be no disagreement. So far as I know that is not claimed. And if it were claimed, it would still be a fact that the cleverest philosophers in their calmest moments have thought they were intuiting value when they were actually reacting passionally. And if the relation between value intuition and passional reaction is so close as that, it seems very likely that the realists may be mistaken in thinking that there is a class of value-judgements which are not expressions of subjective response.

2. As Descartes and Locke argued about the credibility of sense perception, it might be maintained that God created us with the power to intuit values; and God is good (and therefore not deceitful); hence when we are genuinely intuiting value we must usually be right. But if the goodness of God is a guarantee of the reliability of our intuitions, the absolute goodness of God should guarantee their infallibility. Hence the admitted fact of occasional error is, on this argument, incompatible with the absolute goodness of God. (Locke similarly destroyed his argument from the trustworthiness of God to the objectivity of the external world, by questioning the objectivity of secondary qualities.)

The belief that our intuitions of value are usually right, or are likely to be right when there is a large measure of agreement, is simply a-logical faith. For it has no basis of antecedent probability.

But if there is no reason for the belief that particular intuitions of the presence of value are generally reliable, it is equally an a-logical act of faith on the part of a few philosophers to assert that their intuitional acquaintance with the nature of Value in general is likely to be correct, in view of the fact that most philosophers are unable to discover in themselves any such acquaintance. Hence the theory that values are objective qualities of things, independent of the relations of value-bearers to valuing minds, rests upon an a-logical and non-provable basis. While the fact of error and the absence of a criterion of knowledge makes that basis quite unstable.

We are not justified in asserting the objectivity of any entity unless we have a criterion by which to distinguish true and false judgements about it, or unless there is uniformity (absence of inconsistency) among the judgements of mankind. Without this proviso each person could create from his own inventive fantasy an entirely imaginary universe alongside the one we know. There is no such general conformity about value judgements and there is no criterion (as in the case of sense-perception) by which to distinguish true from false intuition.[1] Russell realises this difficulty, but offers only the pious hope that "people probably differ very little in judgements of intrinsic value".[2] Where they do differ he admits a deadlock. But the existence of such a deadlock is not merely an unfortunate difficulty besetting the practical study of the distribution of value; it strikes at the roots of the theory of the objectivity of values. As Professor Laird writes, "the difference between maintaining that there is beauty although no one can ever

---

[1] Compare, for instance, H. Calderwood's eleven "first principles"; Martineau's table of "springs of conduct"; Henry More's twenty-three "noemata moralia"; the "intuitions" of Moore, Laird, Sorley, Scheler, etc., etc.

[2] "Elements of Ethics", p. 43, etc.

know when he has found it, and that there is no such thing as beauty, is so slender that it is not worth quarrelling over". Realism about Value can find no criterion by which to distinguish between logical certainty and psychological certitude. Where there is no criterion of objectively certain knowledge, we *may* be dealing with an objective and independent reality, but we cannot know that it is so: and it is rather futile to assert it.

In answer to this argument it is alleged that the faculty for intuiting value (or, generally, the moral conscious-ness) is liable to development. I do not think this is a satisfactory answer.

In the first place it would be necessary to prove that development proceeds from relatively haphazard in-tuitions towards increasing perspicacity and therefore conformity. This does not seem to be the case. Indeed there appears to be far greater empirical conformity of ethical standards in primitive than in highly civilised communities. "For the real savage of today—and I have no doubt that the same held good of the ancient cave man—is not so much the antithesis as the embodiment of conventionality.... He is a purist who puts manners on a par with morals, and rates impropriety as equivalent to sin."[1] It might be argued of course that in primitive society all individuals are more or less at the same stage of development, while civilised societies are composed of individuals belonging to many different levels. And that the apparent increase in diverse and incompatible value intuitions in higher civilisations is due to that fact. It would be a difficult proposition to verify, but cannot be denied to be possible.

[1] R. R. Marrett.

But secondly, it must be shown that the idea of development is adequate to account for inconsistencies of judgement about intrinsic value. (a) Development certainly implies change in the nature of the objects valued. From being material, private or parochial they become universal, social and ideal. The savage prizes valour, and murder as a sign of devotion to the welfare of the tribe. The more developed moral consciousness prizes humanity or devotion to mankind in general. Looking back from a new standpoint upon the primitive valuation, the civilised and spiritualised man sees that it was directed to an object which is essentially a constituent in a wider whole, and condemns it accordingly. Thus, with some exercise of ingenuity, the apparent inconsistency is explained away: the objects valued are not the same. But if the universalisation of the value-object is able to account for many apparent inconsistencies in the history of moral valuation, there admittedly remain real inconsistencies which cannot be so treated. It can sometimes explain away, but it can never explain. (b) Development as opposed to change is not mere wayward process, but follows a definite principle. Development is the progressive increase in the power to detect shades of difference. The more developed sense draws distinctions where the less developed sense sees only sameness. An individual at a stage of development D_1 detects, we will suppose, in a certain sphere, three degrees of value A, B, C. In his judgement any member of the B-class has more value than any member of the A-class and less value than any member of the C-class; and the members of each class have the same degree of value. An individual at a later stage of development will detect differences of value within these classes—*i.e.* he will judge "a_1" to be less valuable than "a_2", "b_3" to be less valuable than "b_4", etc. But this does not involve inconsistency with the judgements of D_1—merely a more subtle perception of distinctions. But if D_2 judges an "a" to be more valuable, or a "c" to be less valuable, than a "b", that does involve inconsistency. And the inconsistency is *not* accounted for by the supposed development from D_1 to D_2.

The development argument is, I think, at any rate on the present evidence, quite inadequate to the facts.[1] And it must be admitted that a subjective or naturalistic theory of value accounts for the diversity of valuations, which so far is a very real difficulty which an objective theory must face.

I have now said what I think ought to be said about Realism as a pure theory about Value, but before examining it as a theory of Ethics I have to say a few words about the phrase "oughtness to exist", which is commonly used by realists as a synonym of "intrinsic Value".[2] "Ought", so long as it is significant at all, is a *relational* property. When used in ethics it is a normative relation subsisting between moral beings and other objects. When used in value-theory it is a relation subsisting between "existence" and objects; thus "the

[1] If pressed, this argument would only transfer ultimate conflicts of valuation to ultimate conflicts about stages of development. It would, for instance, be difficult to bring order into the conflicting valuations of Gautama Buddha, Confucius and Jesus Christ, as these are interpreted by their respective disciples, by assigning them to different levels of development!

[2] "When we predicate worth or value we assert or imply that the object is worth being or ought to exist." Sorley, op. cit. p. 77. Cf. Moore, "Principia", p. 17, etc.

notion of value always implies a relation to existence".[1]
A further relation between value and existence was, I
believe, first pointed out by Meinong and has been
accepted by the Realist school of thought.[2] Like perceptual qualities, value can only belong to particular
existents. Value-judgements are concerned only with
things as existing. "The mere concept unless realised in
fact is neither good nor evil: it is only as so realised, or
on the assumption of its realisation, that it is called
either."[3] Hence an existing thing, having value, has also
"oughtness to exist"; and that is a relation to its own
existence. In view of this Croce has maintained that all
positive value-judgements are tautologous and all negative
value-judgements are logical contradictions.[4] In reply it
is said that Value is not a *natural* property. But this
reply seems to be irrelevant. For so long as it is a
relational quality it postulates a relation; and the relation
it postulates is between an existing thing and its own
existence. Hence this notion of intrinsic value *must*
necessitate the logical abstraction of the existence of a
thing to stand as one term of the relation "oughtness",
while the existing thing stands as the other term. It is
sensible to assert that if a given state of affairs which
exists or does not exist were to cease or begin to exist,
other things remaining as they are, there would be more
or less value in the whole universe. But it is not sensible
to posit any relation at all between an existing thing and
its own existence.

[1] Sorley, op. cit. p. 78.
[2] "Untersuchungen zur Werttheorie", p. 16. Cf. Urban, "Journal of
Philosophy", xiii, 499 ff.
[3] Sorley, op. cit. pp. 76–77.
[4] "Logos", i, 73. Sorley, op. cit. p. 77.

If the notion of "oughtness to exist" leads to logical confusion, it becomes doubly ambiguous when "ought" is also used, as it must be used, in ethics. The ethical "ought" as defined in non-naturalistic theories is an absolute normative relation subsisting between a particular moral agent and a state of affairs other than that moral agent. Value (*i.e.* in the realists' theory), if it is a relation at all, is not a relation between a thing and anything other than that thing.

The ethical relation may be generalised as follows: every moral agent *ought* always to act in such a way that the total ultimate consequences of his action will be more valuable than would have been the total ultimate consequences of any other action which he could then have voluntarily performed. In other words, moral obligation is directly determined by the valuableness of the states of affairs consequent upon moral actions. This is generally admitted, but we look in vain for any logical connection between Value and moral obligation. The proposition "X-like things have value" implies that if an X-like thing were to begin to exist, other things remaining as they are, there would be more value in the universe than there was before that thing existed. From this it follows that if I were to act in such a way as to cause an X-like thing to exist, other things remaining as they were, there would be more value in the universe than there was before my action. But that does not logically entail the proposition "I ought to act in such a way as to cause an X-like thing to exist", even presuming that I could voluntarily act in this way or refrain from acting in this way. There is no connection of logical entailment between intrinsic value and moral obligation. In order to procure a connection, the proposition "moral agents ought always to act in such a way that the total ultimate consequences of their actions will be more valuable than would have been the total ultimate consequences of any other action which they could then have voluntarily performed" is asserted. It is asserted on the ground of immediate intuition.[1]

Once more we are brought up against direct intuition, and argument is blocked. It should, however, be noticed that this intuition differs in important particulars from the former two intuitions introduced into the theory. As the perception of one patch of yellow is sufficient to make us familiar with the quality Yellow, so the intuition of one case of value in an existing object would be sufficient to make us familiar with the quality Value. And as the distribution of yellowness in the region of existence must be discovered by the examination of each particular existent separately, and there can be discovered no logical law entailing the presence of yellow in members of any class of things except the class of yellow things; so the distribution of value must be discovered by inspection of particular existents. The law, however, which is postulated to connect moral obligation and intrinsic value is a *general* principle asserted to be valid of *all* particular instances of moral obligation. Yet it is not asserted on the ground of empirical inspection of particular instances of moral obligation (that would be impossible, if only because the total ultimate consequences of no human action are known), but is

[1] There is an interesting discussion of this point by H. A. Prichard, in "Mind", January, 1912.

asserted to be valid necessarily of all particular moral actions. The intuition of a necessary universal proposition is a very different thing from intuition of qualities in particular existents. It finds an analogy in the ultimate propositions of logic, which are known to be true intuitively. No sleight of hand in the substitution of "oughtness to exist" for "intrinsic Value" can cover the necessity for this third act of intuition in the Realistic theory in order to bring the theory of Value into connection with ethics, or render that intuition less arbitrary.

Intuitions can be denied or ridiculed; they can be disputed only on the score that they involve consequences which are logically disastrous. As I considered this alleged intuition, I found among its consequences one which is, it seems to me, peculiarly embarrassing, if not logically deplorable. Moral obligation is concerned with the voluntary actions of moral agents. Actions inevitably bring into existence states of affairs which did not exist before the action was performed and would not have existed had the action not been performed. Hence moral obligation envisages states of affairs which do not exist at the time when the moral agent is said to be morally obliged to act in such a way as to cause them to exist. That it is or is not my duty now to act in such a way as will produce a certain state of affairs is an actual fact. According to the theory outlined, that fact is conditioned by the relation between the intrinsic valuableness of the state of affairs in question and the intrinsic valuableness of all the other states of affairs severally which I might then have produced by my voluntary actions. Now it must be remembered that it is an axiom of Realism that only existing things have value.

Hence the actual fact of my moral obligation is conditioned by a non-existent quality which *would* exist if I were to act as I am morally obliged to act. Now I find the notion of a necessary connection subsisting between an actual fact and the relation between qualities which non-existing states of affairs would possess were they to exist, but which they cannot possess except as existing, a logical conundrum impossible for me to solve. It is, in my opinion, sufficient to cast the utmost suspicion upon an intuition which most philosophers confess themselves, on direct inspection, not to possess. But if it is repudiated there remains no necessary connection between the Realistic theory of intrinsic Value and ethics. And that is, in my opinion, sufficient to cast the utmost suspicion upon the Realistic theory of intrinsic Value.

CHAPTER X

COMPARISON OF PSYCHOLOGICAL AND
REALISTIC THEORIES ABOUT VALUE

THERE is no proof either for psychological or for realistic theories about Value. The appeal to direct inspection can give individual certitude but not logical certainty. It has no validity from one mind to another and cannot solve disagreements. The realists find that they are familiar with an objective quality, not psychologically conditioned, and are immediately acquainted with its intrinsic nature or *quale*, as we are immediately acquainted with the intrinsic nature of a perceived patch of yellow. Their opponents profess themselves unable to detect in their own experience any awareness of this quality. The awareness which is alleged on the one hand, and denied on the other, is immediate or intuitive acquaintance and not mediated knowledge; therefore it cannot be proved or disproved. There is no more ultimate proposition, or more certain factual knowledge, from which it could be demonstrated that there is or is not a property, Value, intrinsic in Moore's sense.

The arguments which have been propounded on either side are either not valid or valid only on the assumption of the position they are meant to prove. They do not, therefore, contribute additional probability to that position. They show only that realism and subjective theories are mutually exclusive, not that either has determinate probability. Both theories are unprovable and irrefutable.

Professor Moore writes: "It is just this... fact... that, on any 'subjective' interpretation, the very same kind of thing which, under some circumstances, is better than another, would, under others, be worse—which constitutes, so far as I can see, the fundamental objection to all 'subjective' interpretations".[1] But this consequence of subjective Value theories is only an objection to them if we already know, or have assumed, that Value is a property which is dependent solely upon the intrinsic nature of the object it characterises and not upon external relations in which that object may from time to time stand with valuers. In other words, it is only an objection if the realistic notion of Value is granted. The answer of subjectivism to the alleged objection has been, in Perry's words: "There is no contradiction in this fact, any more than in the fact that what is above the man in the valley is below the man on the mountain".[2] And the reply is perfectly valid if Value is a relational property. The objection and the reply to it bring out the incompatibility of the realistic and the subjective conception of Value; but no more.

Both parties assume a notion which they feel in their bones to be true. Or, as in fact is often the case, they come to the study of Value with habits of mind already formed and associated with specific metaphysical beliefs. (Thus Mr Russell at one time accepted Moore's realism. But later, after his habits of mind had become more

---

[1] "The Conception of Intrinsic Value" (op. cit. pp. 256–7).

[2] "Present Philosophical Tendencies", p. 334; cp. Santayana, "Winds of Doctrine", pp. 141 ff.; Kriebig ("Archiv f. syst. Philos.", 1912); "Derselbe Gegenstand kann nicht nur für verschiedene Subjekte, sondern auch für das gleiche Subjekt zu verschiedenen Zeiten einmal ein Gut, ein andermal ein Uebel sein...".

definitely naturalistic, he was led by Santayana's criticisms—which contain no logical refutation—to abandon his earlier opinions for a view more positivistic than that of his critic).[1] The assumption from which they start conditions the validity of the arguments. In a word, subjectivism and realism are both dependent upon an initial act of a-logical faith. The faith of realism is frankly stated by Stern—who believes that the "Apriori" or logical foundation of all speculative philosophy is "metaphysischer Glaube"—to be contained in the two propositions "Ich glaube an eine Welt, die zugleich seiend und werthaltig ist" and "Ich suche diese Welt".[2] The faith of subjectivism is illustrated by Somlo in the following sentence: "Es gilt absolut, dass nichts absolut gilt".[3] The creed of subjectivism, although negative in content—or in expression—is no less a positive act of faith than that of realism. The categorical denial that there is intrinsic value is not merely a refusal to make the act of faith proposed by Stern, but is itself a positive belief, which is a-logical because incapable of being demonstrated and not guaranteed by a universal verdict of "inspection".

Subjective theories are apt to carry slightly more conviction than realistic theories because the latter assert, and the former deny, a quality which is admitted to be indefinable. Subjectivism has the kind of cogency which belongs to those who deny the reality of the "ineffable experience" of religious mystics. In neither case does

---

[1] Cf. "Philosophy", p. 23.
[2] "Wertphilosophie" ("System des kritischen Personalismus", iii).
[3] "Das Wertproblem" ("Zeitschr. f. Philos. und philosophische Kritik").

that convincingness rest upon logical foundation. For if the "ineffable experience" can be shown to be the sort of thing that, if it did exist, would not be describable—and this is claimed with plausibility for intrinsic value—the fact that description is not forthcoming speaks for the honesty, and not against the accuracy, of those who assert it to exist. There is, however, this difference between the two cases: mystical experience is the product of exceptional training and unusual disposition (like the—describable—experiences of the sufferer from delirium tremens); and the fact that it falls to the lot of but few to experience it, is no ground for doubting the reliability of the few. But the realist lays no claim to exceptional training or disposition such as might account for the fact that he detects in himself experiences in this respect characteristically different from any which the majority of philosophers think they are able to detect in their own minds.

If subjective theories enjoy a slight advantage in this respect it is neutralised by the fact that they reduce ethics to a positivistic science in the teeth of a very general and persistent belief to the contrary. Psychological theories are quite incurably relativistic. The impossibility of transcending the relativity of value to the individual without introducing a notion inconsistent with a psychological definition of Value is a logical, and therefore a final, impossibility. In practice, however, the individualism of this position is mitigated by the similarity of affective and conational dispositions due to common heredity and traditions, social and educative influences, imitativeness, etc., and by the presence and potency of desires and interests directed towards ideals of social import.

In theory Realism excludes relativity of value. But in practice it would be at least as individualistic in tendency as subjectivism. For my intuitions of value must indeed be right or wrong absolutely; but whether they are right or wrong can neither be demonstrated nor argued about. I am therefore perfectly entitled to hold them to be true in face of opposition, until I myself, by some unexplained transformation, come to believe that they are false. Since the intuition of value is a unique mental faculty, there can be no appeal to common dispositions of feeling and volition.

Realism has several weaknesses peculiar to itself. It depends on three independent acts of intuition. The distribution of value has no necessary connection with the definition of Value. This leaves a logical hiatus and allows disagreement in every particular intuition that is made. (In the psychological theories the distribution of value is necessarily attendant upon emotional and volitional mental states.) Realism then requires the intuition of a necessary and universal connection between Value and obligation in order to link up the theory of Value with ethics. Here again is a logical hiatus, because the necessary connection is not logically entailed by the definition of Value. Psychological theories escape such a hiatus at the expense of reducing ethics to a positivistic science. We have further shown that the connection between Value and obligation said to be intuited by realists is attended by consequences which are logically very dubious. If, then, there were a theory about Value which on the one hand escaped the difficult consequence of complete ethical relativity and, without reducing ethics to a positivistic science, escaped on the other hand the logical hiatuses of Realism, it would be preferable to both theories. It would be preferable to psychological theories because it would not conflict with the general ethical opinion of enlightened commonsense, the opinion which most philosophers at most times hold. And it would be preferable to Realism in respect of greater logical simplicity. I believe that the theory which I have defined as Idealism about Value may prove to have these advantages.

CHAPTER XI

IDEALISTIC THEORIES ABOUT VALUE

THE theories about Value which I have called "Idealistic" define Value in terms of Right or Ought. Brentano writes: "We call something good when the love relating to it is right. That which can be loved with the right love, that which is worthy of love, is good in the widest sense of the word".[1] Mr Urban says: "Sometimes we attribute worth to an object when we mean that it deserves to be valued irrespective of its actual valuation by any person or group of persons. Such value is said to be ideal".[2] The notion "Right" or "Ought" is ultimate, unanalysable, normative, and logically antecedent to particular mental processes. It presupposes only the existence of moral agents and of a universe which can be affected by their actions. Value is defined as the property of being an object towards which moral agents *ought* to experience X-like mental states. Positive Value is the property of being an object towards which moral agents ought to experience positive mental states (desire, approval, etc.) and negative Value is the property of being an object towards which moral agents ought to experience negative mental states (revulsion, disapproval, etc.).

Idealistic theories about Value belong to the group of Non-Naturalistic theories, but they differ from Realism in using only one ultimate and indefinable notion in the

[1] "The Origin of Our Knowledge of Right and Wrong."
[2] "Valuation, etc.", p. 23.

philosophy of Value. They are sufficiently differentiated from Naturalistic theories by the fact that Right is logically antecedent to, and unconditioned by, particular mental processes and is normatively valid for moral agents. They are sufficiently differentiated from Realistic theories by the fact that they define Value in terms of Right. Realism affirms *two* ultimate and unanalysable notions, Intrinsic Value and Right, and a synthetic relation between them. Idealism asserts that the relation between Value and Right is analytical: Value is the quality of being an object related to moral beings by the unique relation Right. Realism holds that the proposition "I ought always to act in such a way as to produce a more valuable rather than a less valuable state of affairs" is significant; Idealism holds that it is tautologous. The distinction between Idealism and Realism about Value has been very generally overlooked. But it is a true and an important distinction. It frees Idealism from the peculiar logical weaknesses of Realism, while enabling it to surmount the complete ethical subjectivity of psychological theories.

Idealism is able to give a perfectly coherent explanation of the incidence of Value in various fields of Reality. Religious Value is the property of being an object towards which it is Right that religious adoration should be directed. Aesthetic Value is the property of being an object for which it is Right that admiring contemplation should be experienced. Ethical Value or Goodness is the property of being an object towards which it is Right that the emotion of approval or the sense of obligation should be directed. Finally, some philosophers have asserted that Truth is the property of being an object towards which it is Right that an attitude of intellectual acceptance should be directed.[1] This last assertion involves metaphysical consequences into which it is not possible in this essay to enter. They are not necessary consequences of Idealism about Value, for we may deny that Truth is Value, while affirming that the apprehension of true propositions as true is a valuable state of affairs (i.e. a state of affairs which it is Right should be an object of aspiration and satisfaction). This coherent explanation of the various "fields" of value is a distinct advantage over other theories.

Some writers have distinguished "natural" and "ideal" values as kinds of Value. But this is illegitimate. A thing is said to have natural value if it is the object of desire, etc.; it has ideal value if it Ought to be an object of valuation. The use of the term "value" in both cases is either non-significant or else it involves the implication that the quality of being an object of desire, etc. and the quality of being an object which Ought to be desired, etc., are determinates under a superordinated determinable. The determinable in question has never been discussed and could not be conceived. Those who hold an Idealistic theory about Value should refuse to countenance the use of "value" in empirical psychology and should restrict it to propositions involving an *a priori* Ought.

Idealism tends to be expounded in terms of objective laws or norms of Right, ultimate and "eternally valid", or independent of actual states of affairs. They apply to moral beings as such independently of individual differences in psychological complexion, and they cover all circumstances to which moral beings may conceivably

[1] E.g. Rauch, "Wahrheit, Wert und Wirklichkeit".

be subjected.[1] It is, perhaps, unfortunate that the words "law" and "norm" must be used in this context. In the natural sciences "law" has acquired the meaning of an empirical generalisation about how things or persons do in fact always behave. An ethical law is a generalised statement of how persons *ought* to behave but don't. (It is significant that no one would dream of affirming an ethical obligation to behave in a way conformable to a psychological law of behaviour—e.g. to desire the pleasant.) The word "normative" is, again, also used of the purely psychological compulsion exerted by an approved ideal upon a person who approves it. The idealists' "norm", however, is both antecedent to and *normative for* approval and its psychological consequences. There are, however, no words which would be less objectionable. "Ought" or "Right" is a notion which is unique not only in its indefinability but also in that it is the only member of the class of non-natural relations. We cannot now regulate language; we can beware of linguistic confusion.

Such, then, is the Idealistic theory about Value. It has suffered more than other theories by incompetent exposition and by a frequent association with Theism and other speculative theories. It is nevertheless perfectly determinate and has, as we have shown, certain definite logical advantages. It now remains to examine the arguments which have been advanced in vindication of its truth. Since it is impossible directly to disprove psychological Naturalism it must be impossible directly to prove Idealism about Value. For Idealism and Naturalism are mutually exclusive positions. It follows

[1] Martineau has discussed the possibility of ethically neutral situations.

that the only form which valid arguments for Idealism could possibly take is to show that empirically verifiable facts of experience presuppose the truth of the Idealistic theory about Value. And this is the form they have in fact taken. They are "transcendental deductions" from admitted facts to their necessary conditions.

The premises from which these arguments derive are, so far as I have been able to discover them, the following:

(1) Moral judgements "claim" objectivity.[1]

(2) Certain emotional states, which do in fact occur, could not occur if Right were not objective.

(3) Effective discussion in ethics does occur and could not occur unless there were objectively valid norms.

These three deductions must be examined in turn.

(1) *Moral judgements claim objectivity.* The phrase, in itself ambiguous, means not only or chiefly that value-judgements are verbally couched *as if* they were about objective facts and not subjective states; but it means that the cultured layman, and the philosopher when he is not philosophising, always *intends* an objective and universally valid proposition when he utters a genuine moral judgement. In other words, all men are "naturally" idealists about Value unless and until their attitude is distorted by antecedent and irrelevant philosophical presumptions. Rashdall says: "We say that the Moral Law has a real existence, that there is such a thing as absolute Morality, that there is something absolutely true or false in ethical judgements, whether we or any number of

---

[1] For convenience in this chapter "objective" will be used in the epistemological sense, to mean "logically antecedent to mental processes" and not merely "presented to the Self" or "over-individual".

human beings think so or not. Such a view is distinctly implied in what we mean by Morality. The idea of such an unconditional, objectively valid, Moral Law or ideal undoubtedly exists as a psychological fact".[1] And Dean Matthews proclaims: "No consensus of human judgement on questions of moral value, however impressive, would fully satisfy our demand for objectivity".[2] It is difficult not to dismiss such utterances as mere petulancy of emotional pleading. The chain of reasoning in them seems to be as follows. (a) I and most men, unless misled by erroneous speculation, have a strong instinctive belief in objective morality, and when we utter genuine moral judgements we seem to be judging propositions about objective and psychologically unconditioned ethical norms. (b) If these objective norms have no reality outside our own imagination, moral judgements are not about what we instinctively believe them to be about. (c) Hence morality, if it is what we and most men instinctively believe it to be, presupposes the reality of objective ethical norms. But this argument has no positive cogency without the assumption that the common instinctive belief in objective ethical norms is true. Logically it guarantees no more than what was *asserted* in the premise, *viz.* the existence of an instinctive and general belief in the objectivity of ethical norms.

(2) *Certain emotional states occur which could not occur were there no objectively valid norms.* I believe that there very probably are certain emotional states, which are from time to time experienced, and which presuppose belief in objective norms absolutely independent of the

[1] "The Problem of Good and Evil", ii, 211.
[2] "Studies in Christian Philosophy", p. 133.

beliefs or inclinations of the experient or of any other person whatever. I am unable to doubt that there are, for instance, certain religious emotions which do not only presuppose belief in the existence of God but also belief in absolute duties towards God. And without the belief the emotions could not exist. It seems to me also highly probable that there are other emotions of this kind, which are not religious.[1] If this be admitted it is convincing demonstration of the *existence* of the belief; but it is no demonstration of the *truth* of the belief. The argument takes a blind and unconfessed leap from the existence of a belief to its truth.

(3) *Controversy and discussion about ethical principles does occur, and could not occur unless there were objectively valid norms.* "The very fact that we take it for granted that it is possible to discuss problems of conduct and to compare ideals of life reveals that we do, implicitly or explicitly, assume an objective standard and refuse to decide such controversies on the ground of personal taste or collective prejudice."[2]

So much apparent confusion has prevailed on this point that it will perhaps not be considered out of place

[1] Kant asserts the existence of a unique feeling which he calls "respect" (Achtung) for moral law as such. It differs generically from all other feelings in that "it is not a feeling 'received' through influence, but is 'self-wrought' by a rational concept, and, therefore, is specifically distinct from all feelings of the former kind, which may be referred either to inclination or fear". It differs from them also because "The 'object' of respect is the 'law' only, and that, the law we impose 'on ourselves', and yet recognise as necessary in itself". ("Fundamental Principles of the Metaphysic of Morals", note on p. 21 of Rosenkranz and Schubert's edition and on p. 20 of Abbot's translation.) If this feeling exists it obviously presupposes 'belief' in objective norms.

[2] W. R. Matthews, op. cit.

to offer a brief summary of the conditions of rational discussion. Discussion, which is not vituperation, the coherent comparison of logically grounded beliefs, which is not persuasive eloquence, is only possible from a basis of agreement. It was the elementary lesson of Socrates that discussion can only begin after the implicit premises of the discutants have been laid bare and a common premise, to which both can subscribe, has been found. Whether or not the premise upon which they decide to agree is true or not, is irrelevant to the possibility of coherent discussion.[1] But if the discutants have no common ultimate premise they have no common ground for argument, and discussion is impossible. Hence it follows that in order that coherent ethical discussion may exist it is necessary only that the discutants should agree provisionally and during the discussion to regard certain propositions as true.

But the argument undoubtedly is meant to assert that discussion takes place between discutants who do not have an attitude of provisional assent to the ultimate propositions upon which the discussion is built, but who have towards them an attitude of assertorical belief. Now there may be agreement upon ultimate propositions and deductions and discussion from ultimate propositions whether those propositions are believed to be ultimately valid or psychologically conditioned, or if they are merely implicit and no conscious theory about their validity is held. It is necessary only that during the discussion and for the purposes of the discussion the ultimate premises on which the discussion rests should not be called into question by any of the discutants. It is not therefore

[1] Cf. Mortimer J. Adler, "Dialectic", pp. 22 ff.

necessary, if there is to be discussion about ethical principles, that the discutants should assume that there are
any epistemologically objective (psychologically unconditioned) ethical norms. But even were it empirically
true (it clearly is not so) that *all* ethical discussion were
accompanied in fact by assertorical belief in the unconditional objectivity of the ultimate ethical premises of
the discussion, this empirical fact would not tend to
prove the truth of the belief. It is unnecessary to repeat
that the inference from the existence of a belief to its
truth is logically invalid. If it were valid then all beliefs
would be true, and contradictory propositions would
each be true.

"Comparison of ideals of life" is a vague phrase which
needs further elucidation. If "ideals of life" means
"beliefs about concrete norms of right conduct", what
has already been said about ethical discussion applies
also to it. But if an "ideal of life" means "intellectual
abstractions of principles of conduct and objects of
aspiration from my ideal Self", then, I think, discussion
about "ideals of life", in contradistinction from juxta-
position, is impossible upon any theory. It is impossible
upon a psychological theory about Value because my
"ideal of life" will be, by definition, the object towards
which my sense of obligation is directed. But there is,
by hypothesis, no principle of obligation or source of
Value transcending personal sense of obligation. Hence
each man's "ideal of life", so long as it remains his "ideal
of life", is the ultimate source of Value and Right for him,
but is not constitutive of Value or Right for *another man*.
There can, however, be discussion of immediate aims
and aspirations on the basis of ultimate ideals—such

discussion as leads to the unification of personality. According to the Idealist theory, on the other hand, ultimate ethical norms are immediately intuited. Their intuition carries with it awareness of their obligation. Now ultimate "ideals of life", in so far as they are not psychological, must be assembled intuitions of objective norms. But what is immediately intuited cannot be discussed. Hence there can be no discussion of ultimate "ideals of life" even on the Idealistic view.

It is a conclusion not to be avoided, that the arguments by which Idealism has been defended are logically puerile, whereas the arguments which have been brought to the defence of Realism and psychological Naturalism have considerable apparent speciousness. Yet it would be a mistake to conclude from this that either of those theories occupies a stronger position than Idealism. For, on the one hand there are no degrees of logical validity, and the latter arguments are unable to guarantee a determinate probability for either Realism or psychological Naturalism; and on the other hand, if, as it is claimed, Idealism represents the natural and instinctive convictions of commonsense ethical thought, that alone forbids its summary dismissal on the negative grounds of the absence of positive proof. For a belief is a psychological fact and does not cease to be a fact by being erroneous. Erroneous beliefs, like all other facts, demand explanation. And a general or universal belief which is asserted to be erroneous clamours with vociferous indignation to be explained as a psychological fact.[1] It is therefore indispensably necessary to examine

---

[1] If Idealism could be shown to be not only a universal and instinctive belief of commonsense, but a belief implied in the notion of a rational

more closely the claim that Idealism is the natural and instinctive belief of non-philosophical civilised men.

When I survey the ethical judgements of mankind, I find that it is generally admitted that I am not obliged to do anything which I could not succeed in doing if I willed to do it. Idealists have recognised that this is true.

Hence they have stated the principle of moral obligation as follows: I ought always to act in such a way as to produce the state of affairs which is most right of those which are in my power to produce by voluntary activity. But if this principle were converted into a definition of Value, Value would become relative. For the capacity of voluntary action varies enormously from person to person and no two persons are quite alike in their capacity. Idealism avoids this result by distinguishing a wider meaning of "ought", in which it is not, and a narrower meaning of "ought", in which it is, limited by the capacities of particular moral agents. "It is important to note and distinguish two different implications with which the word 'ought' is used; in the narrowest ethical sense what we judge 'ought to be' done, is always thought capable of being brought about by the volition of any individual to whom the judgement applies. I cannot conceive that I 'ought' to do anything

being, the position would be strengthened out of all measure. Kant claimed this. He asserts both that ethical norms are not valid for men alone, but for all rational beings as such, and also that the recognition of objective norms as objective and as universally valid is an essential attribute of reason. Unfortunately, however, he uses this as a "premise" and not a position to be proved. The ultimate appeal is still to immediate intellectual intuition.

which at the same time I judge that I cannot do. In a wider sense, however,—which cannot conveniently be discarded—I sometimes judge that I 'ought' to know what a wiser man would know, or feel as a better man would feel, in my place, though I may know that I could not directly produce in myself such knowledge or feeling by any effort of will. In this case the word merely implies an ideal or pattern which I 'ought'—in the stricter sense—to imitate as far as possible."[1] I shall call these the *unconditional* "ought" and the *moral* "ought". Dr Broad says: "Now, so far as I can see, the wider sense of 'ought' reduces to that of right, together with the associated notion that, if the right state of affairs were in the power of anyone to produce, he ought to produce it. Take, *e.g.*, the statement that virtue ought to be rewarded. This means primarily that it is right that virtue should be accompanied by happiness, that the one is fitting to the other. In so far as it means more than this the further implication is that anyone who had it in his power to make the virtuous happy would be under an obligation to do so". I would go farther than this and propose that the unconditional "ought" has reference to an idealised moral being not subject to the specific individual limitations of actual moral beings as we have experience of them, that it has reference to a moral being as such. I would assert, congruently with this suggestion, that the unconditional "ought" is valid only for states of affairs which a moral being could conceivably produce. I join issue with Dr Broad over his example. Instead of asserting that virtue ought to be rewarded, I would assert that moral beings ought to

[1] Sidgwick, "The Methods of Ethics", Book i, chap. iii, § 3.

approve of the rewarding of virtue. The latter proposition seems to me to be significant and true. But I can attach no meaning, independent of such propositions, to the notion of absolute and unconditional "fittingness" between two states of affairs such as virtuous action and consequent happiness. Such propositions seem always to me to contain implied reference to right approval, etc., or else to be vestigial remains of a discarded or unconfessed conception, such as is taught by Ethical Theism, of a universe regulated according to teleological principles. I understand the notion of A's fittingness to B in an organised system which includes A and B; but I can form no intelligible idea of A's fittingness to B when A and B are conceived entirely apart from all other existing things.

We shall recur to the conception of the unconditional "ought" later. We now return to an examination of the claim of Idealism to express the ordinary moral consciousness.[1]

When I continue to survey the ethical judgements of mankind, I find that the principle that I ought always to be guided by the dictates of my Conscience[2] is recognised by commonsense to be a fundamental and unarguable maxim of conduct. The "ought" is objective. It does not merely state an empirical generalisation, that we do in fact approve of conduct that was guided by Conscience and disapprove of conduct that was occasioned by desire

[1] The following discussion has been published in "Mind", xxxix, N.S. No. 155.

[2] I use "Conscience" of that faculty by which we become aware of ethical principles, or the rightness of particular actions, but not of the intellectual application of principles to particular concrete situations or conduct.

or inclination in opposition to Conscience; it affirms an obligation antecedent to psychological approval or disapproval. The meaning of the principle is not, I believe, in dispute. All normally constituted moral beings have an impulse to do what seems to them to be right. They have also many other impulses which may, and often do, conflict with this one. Whenever such a conflict occurs they ought to be motivated by the impulse to do what is right and not by another impulse. That there may be left no possibility at all for ambiguity, I think it wise to observe that it is assumed by commonsense that moral beings always *can* effectively will to do what Conscience indicates to be right. And I am inclined to think that commonsense is right in this assumption, so far as normal human persons are concerned. There are, of course, pathological cases of drug-addicts, habitual drunkards, nymphomaniacs, etc., who appear not to be able effectively to will what their Conscience indicates to be right. If this is so, I think we are justified in denying that they are complete moral agents. But, so far as I can see, in the majority of such cases the ineffective volition is consequent upon desire and not upon clear apprehension of right. At the most, the desire (for release from the bondage to habit) may be partially caused by a residual awareness of the partial atrophy of faculty to apprehend the right. In general, and in respect of all normal moral agents, the power of effective volition to be completely guided by Conscience is presumed, and, I think, correctly presumed. A second caution has been proved not to be wholly unnecessary. The principle that I ought always to be guided by my Conscience carries no implications at all about the place of Authority in ethics.

When the rightness or wrongness of particular actions depends upon their probable consequences ordinary intelligence warns me that I should subordinate my own opinion to a person's whose greater experience renders him more likely to predict those consequences correctly. But even in the sphere of immediate intuitions I may recognise that some other person has a more delicate and incisive apprehension of right and wrong than I myself have. When this is the case my Conscience may indicate that, in certain fields or within certain limits, I ought to subordinate my own immediate intuitions to those of that other person. I do not find in myself the awareness of such a duty, but I can conceive that it might be so in others. I can even conceive that the complete subordination of my own Conscience to an external authority, e.g. the Roman Catholic Church, might be apprehended to be my duty. So long as such subordination depends upon an original act of genuine intuition, which is renewed from time to time, and does not degenerate into a comfortable habit, it is consistent with the principle that I ought always to be guided by Conscience. The question of external Authority belongs to casuistry rather than to pure ethics. Therefore we take the principle that I ought on all occasions to regulate myself by the dictates of my own Conscience, to be a genuine maxim of common-sense ethics.

When I survey still further the ordinary moral judgements of mankind, I find that it is generally admitted that we are sometimes mistaken, even after earnest and sincere examination, about what it is right for us to do. I find also that philosophers who have held objective theories about Right have disagreed in their intuitions of the objective principles of right conduct. It follows that we may believe that conduct is right which is in fact wrong. But the former maxim stated that it is always right for me to do what seems to me upon adequate examination to be right. When the maxim that I ought always to follow my own Conscience is combined with the accredited fact that Conscience may err, we get the disastrous result that cases will arise in which it is right for me to do what is wrong. But this is contradictory. For it cannot be both right and wrong for me to perform the same action. The dilemma is apparent in those practical difficulties in which commonsense is frequently involved and which necessitate practical compromises at the expense of logical consistency. Take, as an extreme illustration, the case of the religious fanatic who was convinced that it was his duty to act in such a way as would cause suffering or death to all people who disagreed with his beliefs about the Deity. Commonsense would regard such action as wrong. But if it were performed from the sole motive of respect for duty, and especially if it were performed in despite of feelings of pity and humanity, commonsense would be in a dilemma. So arises the notion of the worthy though mistaken man.

We see, then, that there is a contradiction at the very basis of commonsense ethics, arising out of the conjunction of an intuitive ethical principle, that I ought always to regulate my conduct by my own Conscience, and a recognised matter of fact, that Conscience may err. Before commonsense can be a sound basis for any system of ethical philosophy it is clear that this contradiction must be solved. I shall first dismiss two preliminary attempts to provide a solution and then I shall suggest the line of thought along which it seems to me that it should be solved.

1. It is natural to investigate the possibility of a solution in the two meanings of "ought". The assertion that Conscience may err presupposes the existence of other objective norms of conduct besides the duty always to act in accordance with Conscience. The contradiction lies in the fact that when I conform my conduct to an erring Conscience my conduct is right in respect of the norm of obedience to Conscience and wrong in respect of another norm. It is suggested that the apparent contradiction may be solved if we use "ought" in different senses when we say "I ought always to obey my Conscience" and when we say that we ought to act in conformity with any of those other objective norms in the intuition of which Conscience may err.

In the wider meaning of "ought" a state of affairs is Valuable towards which moral beings as such ought to experience an X-like attitude. In the sphere of ethics, a state of affairs is Right towards which moral beings as such ought to experience an attitude of approval. In the narrower meaning of "ought" a particular moral being ought (is morally obliged) to produce the most right state of affairs which it is in his power by voluntary activity to produce. The narrower sense of "ought" is simply a limitation of the wider sense, in its application to the states of affairs able to be produced by the voluntary activities of particular moral beings. Let us suppose three states of affairs, A, B, C, such that B is more valuable than A, and C is more valuable than B. We will suppose, further, two moral agents, X and Y, such that

X can produce A, B, or C by his voluntary activity, and Y can produce A or B, but not C, by his voluntary activity. In the wider sense of "ought" both X and Y ought to produce C rather than B or A, and B rather than A. In the narrower sense of "ought" X ought to produce C, and Y ought to produce B. We have difference but not conflict. We do not find that Y ought to produce A although he could produce B or that X ought to produce B although he could produce C. Nor do we ever find that any moral agent ought ever to do what is wrong, although he were able to do it.

The conflict in question is a conflict between duties or specific instances of moral obligation, deriving, on the one side, from intuited norms, and on the other hand from the intuited norm of obedience to Conscience. Now when Conscience errs it either supposes a certain type of action which is wrong to be right or supposes a certain type of action which is less right than another to be more right than another. If it is asserted that this rightness about which it errs is unconditional rightness, it still follows that it will lead to error in respect of moral obligation whenever the state of affairs envisaged in the judgement of unconditional obligation comes within the capacity of a particular moral agent to produce by voluntary activity. And in any case errors of Conscience occur within the field of actions which are morally obligatory. Error cannot be explained away by the two meanings of "ought".

2. Some philosophers have asserted that Conscience is infallible. If this is so, commonsense is wrong in supposing that we can err when we are genuinely intuiting ultimate norms of conduct. Kant has sometimes

been thought to have advocated this view. He did, indeed, hold that when genuine ethical principles are presented to the Pure Practical Reason they are recognised to be true with the same immediacy and certainty as that with which the theoretical Reason recognises ultimate axioms of thought to be true. But these ethical principles are not what we mean by norms of conduct. They are formal properties which all true norms of conduct must possess. Kant did not hold that individual Conscience, when immediately intuiting norms of right conduct, is infallible.[1] And I know no writer who has advanced that supposition with the slightest cogency.

The contradiction in commonsense ethics does not, then, automatically disappear in philosophical Idealism. The question remains whether it is ultimate or whether it can be superseded at a higher level. I will restate the problem more specifically. The statement that Conscience may err presupposes the existence of objective norms of conduct and the notion of an objective norm in commonsense ethics, as in philosophical ethics, involves "the associated notion that if the right state of affairs were in the power of anyone to produce, he ought to produce it". From this it follows that, if I could not do what is most right under the circumstances (e.g. love my enemy), I ought nevertheless to choose the course of action which is most right of those which *are* in my power to produce (e.g. behave towards my enemy as though I loved him). "The most right action which I could do if I willed to do it" is a perfectly determinate notion, and I shall call such an action the *best practicable action*. The

[1] Cf. Broad, "Five Types of Ethical Theory", pp. 122–3.

notion of moral obligation ("ought" in the narrower sense) differs from that of unconditional right ("ought" in the wider sense) in that it does not admit of degrees. We hold that one state of affairs is more right and another less right but that both are right. But we do not hold actual moral obligation to apply in various degrees to various contemplated actions. Whenever I make or could make a moral choice I am absolutely obliged to choose the best practicable action.

But the best practicable action is not necessarily identical with that which I believe to be the best practicable action. For I may be mistaken about what I could do if I willed, and I may be mistaken about what is most right or ethically fitting in the circumstances, or, finally, I may be mistaken about the nature of the circumstances in which I am called upon to act and about the probable consequences of my action. Hence the principle that I ought always to perform the best practicable act seems to conflict with the principle that I ought always to obey my conscience. For I cannot be obliged to two incompatible courses of action unless they are equally right and the choice between them ethically indifferent. Dr Broad co-ordinates the narrower application of "ought" with the latter principle, for he says that it is bound up with the facts that the belief that an action is right is a motive for doing it, and that when this motive is in conflict with other motives it should always win.[1] Yet this motive has admittedly often led men to do actions which are wrong. It seems equally true that I ought always to do the best practicable act, and that I ought always to do what I believe to be the best practic-

[1] Op. cit. p. 166.

able act. The two are not necessarily identical, and if on any occasion they are identical that is a purely contingent fact.

Several modes of solution naturally suggest themselves.

1. It might be maintained that the proposition "I ought always to obey my Conscience" implies that any action the motive of whose performance was the agent's belief that it was the best practicable action, was in fact the best practicable action. And the following argument might be advanced in defence of the seeming paradox. Any state of affairs which contains as a constituent part the voluntary action of a moral being has, as a whole, the ethical characteristic of being Right or Wrong. If, as is often the case, the motive of the agent is the belief that the proposed action is right, or some other motive in conflict with this motive, that fact will be an element in the total state of affairs. And it will itself be intrinsically right or wrong. In all such cases, it might be argued, action from, or in opposition to, Conscience, has this unique characteristic, that it determines the ethical character of the total situation of which it is a constituent part. If this were the case I should always be performing the best practicable act when I am guided by my belief that any action is right, even though that belief were mistaken.[1]

But the postulate on which this contention relies is in opposition to ethical judgements whose truth it would be fantastical to deny. The action of the religious fanatic who endeavours to cause the death of such people as disagree with his views about the nature of God is always wrong, although it may sometimes be conscientious.

[1] Kant asserts negatively that only those actions have positive ethical value the sole motive in the performance of which was Conscience.

And the total situation of which that action is a part is yet more obviously wrong. Again, even though the extreme view were held that the only examples of ethical Rightness are actions of moral beings which are conscientious, it would be possible that certain actions of this kind should tend to lessen the total amount of Rightness in the universe. For they might be "stumbling-blocks" to others, making it less easy for them to act conscientiously, and hence less probable that they would act conscientiously. But it seems obvious that it is my duty to act in such a way as to increase the total amount of rightness in the universe so far as is in my power. And to act in such a way would be to perform the best practicable action. Hence the opposition still remains between the duty to obey Conscience and the duty to perform the best practicable action.

Moreover, if in all ethical situations the ethical value of the motive is alone determinative of the total value of the whole situation, the assertion that one man has more accurate or more obtuse ethical perception than another becomes nugatory. And the duty to endeavour to improve my perception of right and wrong disappears. For I cannot by so doing increase my power to produce ethically valuable situations. Rather, if it is true that it is more arduous to live up to a finely discriminating than to an obtuse sense of right and wrong, the possession of such a sense would render it less likely that I should produce ethically right situations. This contradicts the universal intuitive notions of duty of mankind. And it is illegitimate to supersede one self-evident principle by another, unless the one is seen to be derivative from or contained in the other.

2. It is obvious that if on every occasion I performed the best practicable act I should produce the greatest amount of positive ethical value during my life that I was capable of producing. It is equally obvious that the chances are infinitesimal that by obeying his Conscience any human being will always do the best practicable act. And the chances that he would do so by any other rule of life would seem to be less. But it would seem to be self-evident that any man ought to endeavour to produce a greater amount of ethical value throughout his life, rather than a less amount. And most men would be likely to produce a greater amount by consistently obeying Conscience than by any other rule of life or by adopting no rule. Hence if I ought to produce a greater rather than a smaller amount of ethical value on the whole, I ought consistently to obey my Conscience. The second "ought" is logical. The principle that I ought always to obey my Conscience is a practical rule derived from the ethical and ultimate principle that I ought to produce a greater rather than a smaller amount of positive ethical value on the whole. I do not think that this is opposed to the intuitive ethical convictions of commonsense, but that commonsense does not as a rule succeed in going behind the principle of obedience to Conscience, which it takes as ultimate instead of derived. So long as each ethical situation is taken independently it is impossible to go behind that principle. It is necessary to take the whole life of a moral being as our unit.

The principle "I ought always to do the best practicable act" will, on this view, no longer be a concrete ethical principle involving moral obligation, but an ethical ideal or extrapolation. It simply states that if anyone always performed the best practicable act he would cause a greater amount of positive ethical value throughout his life than under any other circumstances whatever. Or the "ought" means unconditional right, having reference to moral beings as such without mor l obligation upon individual moral beings in every concrete circumstance. It is contradictory to assert that anyone ought *always* to do the best practicable act, for although the definition of "best practicable act" involves that on any particular occasion the agent could perform that act if he willed to do so, we have seen that he could not if he willed render it even likely that he would *always* do the best practicable act. I do not think this conclusion is opposed to anything in commonsense or practical ethical notions. We should rather notice a tendency among philosophers to take an abstract ideal too concretely.

But the initial conflict is not yet completely solved. It is probable that for most men the rule of obedience to Conscience would ensure the greatest amount of positive ethical value on the whole, but in the case of some men a more complicated principle might seem necessary. It is not clear that both the religious fanatic and the humanitarian, both a Nietzsche and a Soloviov, would produce the greatest amount of positive ethical value by following each his own Conscience. In the case of the religious enthusiast, for example, one might suggest that he would produce more value in his life if he made a rule of following Conscience except when it conflicted with the emotions of pity or humanity. No particular rule of this kind could of course be justified. For it would involve setting the ethical convictions of one man, or group of men, above those of another. And there is no more ultimate authority than Conscience itself or ethical conviction by which such a procedure could be justified. But the suggestion has also theoretical difficulties. For commonsense claims to recognise in the maxim "I ought always to obey my Conscience" a *universal* principle. The whole state of affairs involved in the suggested action of the religious fanatic would be generally judged to be disvaluable. But the fact that his action was in obedience to Conscience (which is an element in the whole state of affairs) has positive value. Its rightness is not negatived by the disvalue of the whole of which it is a part. We make such judgements most frequently of a man who knows that his belief about what is right is opposed to the beliefs of most men of his age or country, and follows his own conviction at the expense of odium or unpopularity.

Nor does it help to assert that, when I judge that a certain person was right in that he obeyed his Conscience but wrong in that his Conscience was mistaken, I am making two independent judgements about different objects, the ethical characteristics of his motive and the ethical characteristics of his behaviour. The original dilemma is thereby simply restated. For he was right to do what he believed to be right but what he did was wrong. And our object was to examine the seeming paradox that it is sometimes true that I ought to do what is wrong: since, unless some more ultimate principle can be found, "X is wrong" implies "I ought not to do X"; while the principle that I ought to do what I believe to be right may involve that I ought to do what is really wrong.

8-3

3. We must therefore once more endeavour to widen our ethical vision. In place of the principle "I ought to adopt that rule of conduct which is likely to ensure that I shall produce a greater amount of positive ethical value throughout my life than would be ensured by any alternative rule", I would suggest the larger principle "I ought to adopt that rule of conduct which is likely to ensure that all men present and to come will produce a greater amount of positive value throughout their lives than would be ensured by any alternative rule". The rule of obedience to Conscience was seen not to be indicated by the former principle in all cases, although it was indicated in the great majority of cases, and it was found impossible to decide in particular cases that it was or was not indicated. But it would seem to be indicated in all cases by the wider principle. For, as human nature is constituted, any relaxation of this rule would have far-reaching effects, and would tend to cause it to be neglected in cases where it ought to be adopted. And the impracticability of deciding when it should be supplemented and when strictly followed tends to the same conclusion. For the only alternative to its universal adoption is the majority vote. And that would suppress ethical geniuses as well as ethical degenerates. The argument of course presupposes that Conscience is on the whole a veridical faculty, and that general changes in ethical beliefs are on the whole towards greater truth rather than towards greater falsity. But this assumption must be common to all serious ethical theories.

If we are right, the paradox cannot be solved by any theory of ethics which takes the particular ethical situation or the single individual as its unit for discussion.

It is necessary to take as the ultimate unit for ethics the notion of mankind as a single ethical substance, composed of separate ethical subjects standing in ethical relations to each other and to the universe, and ethically progressive.

From this point of view the contradiction in commonsense ethics is superseded. The maxim "I ought always to do the best practicable act" (which was seen to be contradictory in itself) is abandoned in favour of the wider maxim "I ought to adopt that rule of conduct which is most likely to ensure that I and all men, present and to come, will produce a greater amount of positive value throughout our lives than would be ensured by any alternative rule". From this maxim we *derive* the practical rule "each man ought always to be guided by his Conscience". The "ought" in the latter rule is analogous to the logical meaning of "ought" which we employ when we say that a man ought to be consistent about an end or aspiration which he does in fact take as ultimate for himself.[1] But it differs from the ordinary logical application of "ought" in that the end to which it is referred is absolute and objectively valid for all moral agents.

I do not believe that there is anything in this analysis which is not implicit in the elementary and unanalysed moral judgements of commonsense. Nor do I believe that it contains anything which could be objected to on the grounds of commonsense.

On this assumption we will turn again to the claim of the Idealist to represent in philosophy the natural and instinctive ethical convictions of commonsense. In

[1] Cf. Broad, op. cit. pp. 162–3.

view of the commonsense axiom that I should always act in such a way as my own Conscience would approve, Idealism is compelled to remodel its definition of moral obligation ("ought" in its narrower meaning). Yet when we look more closely we see that it needs to *recast* only, and not to remodel. The "best practicable action" is a definite notion and is recognised by commonsense to be a significant and necessary notion. But as men are constituted, and with their actual limitations of insight and ability, the act which is conscientious is, from the widest and only consistent point of view, identical with the best practicable act. Commonsense has instinctively discovered an empirical rule for the performance of the best practicable act, and that rule does not nullify or remodel the notion of ethical obligation but renders it more concrete in its application to actual moral beings.

Commonsense, however, is not content with human beings as they are; it envisages a gradual process of improvement and a gradual conquest of limitations. It also regards every moral being as obliged, so far as rests in his power, to further that process. This presumption logically entails the postulation of Values which are prior to and valid for actual aspirations and beliefs about value. Idealism postulates such Values, which are independent of actual human valuations. It postulates Values, however, which are in relation to the notion of a moral being as such, and that means Values which could conceivably be realised by moral beings. Here too it is close to commonsense. For commonsense has never been at home with the notion of Value which is wholly unrelated to moral agents and which exists in complete independence of human aspirations. Its Ultimate Value has always been a Value realisable by the ideally perfect being.

The conformity to commonsense presumptions does not, of course, constitute a guarantee. It is a point worthy of investigation only when intellectual verification has failed. But a psychological fact, as we have said above, remains a fact even though it be proved an erroneous belief. If, then, a belief or assumption is asserted to be erroneous it should still be explainable as a psychological fact. This becomes important when the assumption is very general, very persistent, and unconsciously utilised before being consciously defined.

When Dr Tennant is discussing Non-Natural theories about Value he suggests that the "empty concept" of Absolute Value was reached by intellectual abstraction from every concrete conditioner of Value and subsequent hypostatisation of the bare *form* of the Value-relation which was left. This might be true of philosophers of whom it was true that the notion of absolutely unconditioned Value had first been reached by them after philosophising. As an explanation of a universal presumption of commonsense it is irrelevant. Commonsense does not intellectually abstract and hypostatise its abstractions. Its thought is practical and concrete. When it transcends the world of experienced fact, it does so in virtue of an impulse which impels to imaginative and not intellectual construction. If, also, the philosophers may have obtained their conscious belief in Absolute Value by intellectual clarification of an unconscious presumption of commonsense, Dr Tennant's "explanation" of this as hypostatisation of an intellectual abstraction from an experienced fact loses much of its force.

A more relevant explanation of the commonsense presumption (and it is *this* which clamours for explanation) is the perseverance in the adult of the psychological habits of childhood. As children we are trained in the acceptance of rules and obligations which are then absolute for us. The "must" of the child, however paltry it be, is unconditional in the highest sense, less because of the limitations of the child's own comprehension than because of the indolence of the educators, which impels them ever to tread the more easy path. So, it might be argued, having learnt in childhood obedience to norms which originated we knew not where, as adults we create for ourselves norms which originate nowhere at all. That, and the vulgar instinct to impose *our own* ideals as obligatory upon our neighbours, might conceivably be the psychological explanation of the civilised man's belief in objective ethics.

But when we contemplate the human race more at large this explanation appears frivolous. We see a fundamental psychological disposition to objectify those aspirations and ideals which have been paramount for each age and nation. This impulse, most surprisingly vital in primitive races, has been one of the essential factors of religion in development and has been a very important motive in speculative philosophies. We see the continuance and the authority of ideals wax and wane with faith in the imaginative constructs with which they were associated; we see changing ideals seizing hold upon and breathing new life into faded and lifeless constructs; we see that process in the human race which the Non-Naturalist calls progress and the Naturalist calls linear change, everywhere dependent upon the belief that mankind is struggling towards the apperception and realisation of Values which are independent of himself as he now is. The explanation by "childhood's memories" when applied to this fact has an altogether too simple credulity. This fact is ultimate for the psychologist; it is incapable of *psychological* explanation.

The intellectual convincingness of facts like the above must vary considerably from mind to mind. Their degree of cogency cannot be objectively assessed. The danger is that they be allowed too much influence when they act unconsciously and that they be rejected too summarily when they have been consciously apprehended. We do not, therefore, attempt to define the degree of certitude which they *ought* to awake. So long as we are discussing objective philosophy we remain at the assertion that Idealism is very close to a general commonsense presumption, which is intimately linked with an ultimate human impulse, while subjective theories entail conclusions which are always and inevitably paradoxical to commonsense.

It now remains to examine the *application* of Idealism. It is in its application that the psychological theory is peculiarly strong; having reduced the Philosophy of Value to empirical psychology it is necessarily watertight here. It has, in fact, simply to examine, and, unless it impedes itself by adopting an initial definition which limits it unnecessarily, there is nothing to apply. But with Idealism, which is not an empirical science, the application must be investigated in principle and outline.

CHAPTER XII

APPLICATION OF IDEALISM

W E must be careful to guard against the supposition that the definition of Value in relation to moral beings as such involves a subjective definition of the so-called Values of Beauty and Truth.

Aesthetic Value was defined as the property of being an object for which it is Right that admiring contemplation should be experienced. It is possible that this may be a definition of Beauty. But it is not essential that it should be so. Beauty may be, and I think that it is, a formal property of beautiful objects, as independent of appreciation or perception as are colours and shapes. When we say that a wood-engraving by Bewick is beautiful and an illustration in a current weekly paper is not beautiful, we are asserting that the former possesses, and the latter does not possess, certain relations of balance and harmony (what the Japanese call *notan*) between the masses of whites and greys, in virtue of which the picture has coherence and unity. These relations are more subtle than, but objective in the same way as, such relations as "being to the right of", "being in the middle of", etc. The perception of beauty is really perception of a special class of objective formal relations among primary and secondary sense-qualities. If this is so, then every material object either has or has not beauty. The Idealist who held this view about Beauty would not assert that "being beautiful" means "being an object towards which admiring contemplation ought to be felt"; but he would assert that as a matter of fact admiring contemplation ought to be felt towards objects which are beautiful. I think he might also assert that objects which are beautiful ought to be created by moral agents rather than objects which are not beautiful. If he asserts this he brings aesthetics within the sphere of ethics.

Thus, whether Beauty is held to be an intrinsic or a subjective quality, "aesthetic value" is not a peculiar kind of Value but is a term used merely to indicate the application of Value to a particular class of value-objects.

"Truth" has been regarded as a kind of Value by some Idealists. They assert that when we say a proposition is true we mean that rational beings ought to adopt an attitude of intellectual acceptance towards it. Others have asserted that Truth is not a kind of Value but that the apprehension of true propositions as true is a valuable state of affairs (i.e. one which moral beings ought to endeavour to produce). I think we can go beyond the latter assertion without necessitating the peculiar metaphysical consequences which are entailed by the former. Without discussing what we do mean when we say that a proposition is true, an Idealist might assert that we do not mean that rational beings ought to adopt an attitude of intellectual acceptance towards it. He could then add that as a matter of fact we ought (in the wider sense of "ought") to adopt an attitude of intellectual acceptance towards propositions which are true. It would then follow that every moral agent ought (in the narrower sense of "ought") to cultivate and promote the intellectual acceptance of true propositions as true, to the extent of his capacity to do so.

"Religious values" presuppose the existence of a

supernatural object of religious faith. The Idealist who was a Theist would assert an unconditional obligation to perform certain actions (e.g. worship the Deity) and to experience certain emotions (e.g. religious adoration). The Idealist who was not a Theist would differ from the former in not asserting an obligation to perform actions which imply, or to experience emotions which presuppose, belief in the existence of a Deity. A difficulty arises when religious emotions are recognised to be good by those who do not hold religious beliefs. For if "good" is meant strictly, it means "worthy to be experienced" and states an (unconditional) obligation on moral beings to experience emotions which are good. It must, however, be remembered that the difficulty arises only in respect of specifically religious emotions, i.e. emotions which could only be experienced towards the idea of an existing supernatural object of faith. These emotions are admitted to be rare and to be acquired only after much labour and mental discipline. The Idealist who is not a Theist must deny that they are good (because they presuppose the intellectual acceptance of a false proposition as true), though he may on other grounds and in other respects find positive value in the persons who experience them. From the conviction that specifically religious emotions are good some people have been led to accept the beliefs which those emotions presuppose. And I think that, upon an Idealistic theory about Value, this is a very strong argument for Theism *if the premise is granted that specifically religious emotions are good*.

"Moral value" has been defined. It indicates the application of Value to possible conduct. Actions are

usually said to be good or bad in view of their obligatoriness or non-obligatoriness. But they are also value-
objects in the same sense that beautiful or non-beautiful
objects are value-objects. For they are appropriate
objects of the emotions of approval and disapproval.
And the Idealist asserts the obligation to approve of good
conduct and disapprove of bad conduct.

I can find no property which is not moral Value but
which is a universal concomitant of moral Value, as
Beauty is not aesthetic Value but is a universal concomitant of aesthetic Value. Some philosophers have
asserted that there is an unanalysable relational quality of
Fittingness, which is a universal concomitant of moral
Value because whatever is fitting ought to be produced
by moral agents if they can produce it. But I am inclined to think that those philosophers who have
believed that they could detect an unanalysable quality
"Fittingness", logically antecedent to moral obligation,
were really aware of a property, analogous to Beauty,
which I will call the harmonious interrelation of the
constituents of an organised whole. We detect a relation
of fittingness between two lines or two masses in a
picture; but that fittingness only belongs to them as
elements in the picture. Were the rest of the picture
deleted and they alone left, the fittingness by which they
were before seen to be related would disappear. So
when we seem to detect the fittingness of virtue com-
mensurately rewarded we are really detecting the
fittingness of two elements in an organised system. That
system is a universe organised on teleological principles.
The mistake arises, I think, in the following way. When
I look at a picture and observe the fittingness of two

masses in it, I concentrate my attention almost entirely upon those two masses but retain the idea of the picture in the background of my memory. If the perception of the fittingness of the two masses is to remain vivid it must be continually refreshed by the vision of them in the whole of which they are constituents. But if I carry the process of abstraction still farther and blot out the rest of the picture completely, or place another picture in its stead, the fittingness of the two masses is lost. So when I contemplate virtue and commensurate reward in abstraction I see them to be fitting because I have the idea of an organised universe in the background of my mind. But I do not see that their fittingness is conditional upon their position in an organised universe because I cannot wholly free my mind from the idea of an organised universe. Nor can I imagine an entirely different universe which contains virtue and reward. I can idealise the actual universe (as I can imagine a better picture than the one I see) but I cannot imagine no universe or an entirely different one.

We must now examine the notion of an idealised moral being, or a moral being as such, in relation to which things are said to have value. This conception is not to be confused with the "ideal Self" of the psychologist. That is a concrete psychical fact, which varies from individual to individual. It is limited according to the capacities of the individual—or at least according to his apprehension of his own capacities. I might wish to possess a cultivated aesthetic taste but I could not *aspire* to possess a cultivated aesthetic taste if I believed myself constitutionally unable to differentiate beautiful from non-beautiful objects. The notion of a moral being as such, on the other hand, is an intellectual construct designed to transcend the differences of individual capacity.

A moral being as such must have the power of real moral choice among actions which effectively influence a universe outside himself. He must possess the power to apprehend true propositions as true, to appreciate and create beautiful objects, to experience emotions, such as love, enjoyment of friendship, pity, approval, etc., which we term valuable, and (perhaps) the capacity to experience religious emotions. He will possess each of these qualities in the highest possible degree and will not be hampered by the practical impossibility, with which all actual moral beings are familiar, of enjoying and cultivating all of these faculties conjointly in the highest possible degree.

The *existence* of an ideal moral being is a matter to be decided by metaphysics and does not come within the province of theory of Value. A metaphysic which held such a being to exist would be either Spiritualistic Absolutism or Theism. I hesitate to think that it is impossible that such a being should exist; but I am certain that whenever he has hitherto been conceived as existing he has been imagined either too vaguely or too abstractly to be useful for the purposes of theory of Value. But the notion of an idealised moral being serves the purpose of the theory of Value without the presumption of his existence.

The norms of right conduct in terms of which Idealism is usually and conveniently stated are, like the laws of natural science, really generalisations of specific instances of obligation. Every ethical situation, that is every situation in which a specific moral agent is faced with an actual choice between specific actions, is unique. It can never be *wholly* brought under general laws. In every such situation the capacity of the agent to perform the best possible action is limited in two ways; first by his capacities, mental and physical, and secondly by the acuteness of his perception of right and wrong (because we have seen that, when the ultimate consequences of moral conduct are taken into consideration in their widest extension, the best practicable act is always identical with the act performed under the guidance of Conscience). Obedience to Conscience is a practical rule ensuring the performance of the best practicable act. But were the agent less impeded by those limitations, and were his Conscience more veridical, he would have been able to act better than he could in fact act; and were he completely unhampered, were he an ideal moral agent, he would be able to perform the absolutely and unconditionally right action in the specific circumstances. It is precisely the significance of such statements as these that Idealism is concerned to maintain. Idealism asserts that in every ethical situation there is a Right which is not relative to individual beliefs or emotions (subjectivism), and, further than this, which transcends the actual moral obligation inherent in the situation and is not relative to the Conscience and capacities of the agent. So we assert that a certain moral agent would, had he been free from certain actual limitations, have been able to perform conduct more valuable than the most valuable conduct which he could in fact perform. And this is asserted as an objective fact, true of all concrete ethical situations. If less than

this is asserted it is impossible to escape ultimate individualism of Value, and ethics will become a branch of
sociology.

There is, indeed, a vigorous movement in contemporary philosophy advocating an empirical treatment of
ethics. Ethics, it is said, is a branch of sociology, and
only by empirically investigating concrete ethical situations and actual moral judgements can we hope to reach
any useful conclusions about conduct.[1] I am wholly in
agreement with the claim that useful knowledge about
what conduct is good and what conduct is bad must be
obtained empirically. But that claim is not at variance
with Idealism. Idealism not only admits of, but needs to
be completed by, an empirical science of morals. For
although it holds that knowledge of intrinsic right and
wrong is intuitive and immediate, and that individual
Conscience is the ultimate authority for the individual,
it does not hold that individual Conscience is fixed and
unchangeable. Development in the capacity to apprehend value is a normal and natural event, dependent like
aesthetic perception upon cultivation and practice. The
empirical investigation of morals is a valuable pro-
paedeutic to the training of individual Conscience.
Idealism does assert, and subjectivism denies, that this
empirical investigation may lead to a juster and truer
apprehension of objective facts. Apart from Idealism, or
a similar Non-Natural theory about Value, the empirical
science of morals is a natural science about human facts,
purely and simply a branch of sociology, and leads to no
knowledge beyond the knowledge of the empirical facts
which are its immediate data.

[1] John Dewey is the most extreme advocate of this view.

The problem of the validity of Value-judgements, with which we have been solely concerned is not, and could not be, of any direct use to a moral being desiring guidance in concrete ethical situations. Whether or not the energy spent by philosophers upon speculation which has no direct practical utility be misspent is a question quite outside the scope of the present enquiry. If it should be condemned as a serious occupation, it may yet, perhaps, be tolerated as a harmless recreation.

For EU product safety concerns, contact us at Calle de José Abascal, 56–1°,
28003 Madrid, Spain or eugpsr@cambridge.org.